"Schuchardt admirably integrates the histo
nology with a rich understanding of Christ
Postman in one hand and the Bible and Chr
he offers a thoughtful and challenging persp
media today."

Douglas Groothuis, Professor of Philosophy, Denver Seminary; author, *The Soul in Cyberspace*

"Read Schuchardt has been doing groundbreaking work in the new academic field of media ecology. Like his mentor, Neil Postman, he is asking us to think critically about the impact that new technology is having on everything from human development to political discourse to spiritual formation. This is an important book that is a must-read for serious Christians. I highly recommend it."

Terry L. Johnson, Senior Minister, Independent Presbyterian Church of Savannah; author, *The Family Worship Book*; *Worshipping with Calvin*; and *Serving with Calvin*

"Read Schuchardt's progenitor is Marshall McLuhan, whose pithy style he so well channels. I once observed Read in the classroom as students both giggled and squirmed in their seats. They giggled because they were overjoyed that someone understood their world. They squirmed because he put his finger on what they had not yet perceived about the digital age. For the student of communication there is gold to be found in this hill of wise counsel."

Arthur W. Hunt III, Professor of Communications, The University of Tennessee, Martin

"Read Schuchardt shaped the way I think about technology more than anyone else. With technology changing at an ever-increasing pace, Schuchardt is a sure guide to not only keeping your sanity but also your soul, whichever side of the Tiber you're on."

Brantly Millegan, Founder and Editor in Chief, ChurchPOP

"Schuchardt's *Media, Journalism, and Communication* is a publisher's nightmare and a reader's dream. It fits no pre-established publishing category, because it is entirely too insightful to do so; its wine will not fit those wineskins. If Marshall McLuhan had been intelligible, Neil Postman a Christian, and Jacques Ellul an American, this is the book they would have coauthored (with Wendell Berry as their editor), though they would have taken ten times as many pages to have done so."

T. David Gordon, Professor of Religion and Greek, Grove City College, Grove City, Pennsylvania

"Not only has Schuchardt made the case for why the communication arts are essential to the liberal arts, he convincingly explains how they can make us better humans. This is one of the most superb short books ever written on the role and effect of media, and a must-read for every Christian college student."

Joe Carter, Editor, The Gospel Coalition; contributor, *NIV Lifehacks Bible*

"Read Schuchardt is in the business of telling fish about the water they swim in. We 'fish' instinctively breathe, eat, and drink media in all forms, all the time. We hardly notice. Schuchardt helps us notice both the fascinating and alarming. Schuchardt says some crazy things about media that just happen to be true, while pointing to truths in the gospel that may strike us as crazy. It's why he is such a good person to discuss the media water we swim in."

Mark Galli, Editor in Chief, *Christianity Today*

**MEDIA, JOURNALISM,
AND COMMUNICATION**

+ RECLAIMING THE CHRISTIAN INTELLECTUAL TRADITION

David S. Dockery, series editor

CONSULTING EDITORS

Hunter Baker
Timothy George
Neil Nielson
Philip G. Ryken
Michael J. Wilkins
John D. Woodbridge

OTHER RCIT VOLUMES:

Art and Music, Paul Munson and Joshua Farris Drake
Christian Worldview, Philip G. Ryken
Ethics and Moral Reasoning, C. Ben Mitchell
The Great Tradition of Christian Thinking, David S. Dockery and Timothy George
History, Nathan A. Finn
The Liberal Arts, Gene C. Fant Jr.
Literature, Louis Markos
The Natural Sciences, John A. Bloom
Philosophy, David K. Naugle
Political Thought, Hunter Baker
Psychology, Stanton L. Jones

MEDIA, JOURNALISM, AND COMMUNICATION
A STUDENT'S GUIDE

Read Mercer Schuchardt

WHEATON, ILLINOIS

Media, Journalism, and Communication: A Student's Guide

Copyright © 2018 by Read Mercer Schuchardt

Published by Crossway
    1300 Crescent Street
    Wheaton, Illinois 60187

Cover design: Jon McGrath, Simplicated Studio

First printing 2018

Printed in the United States of America

Trade paperback ISBN: 978-1-4335-3514-7
ePub ISBN: 978-1-4335-3517-8
PDF ISBN: 978-1-4335-3515-4
Mobipocket ISBN: 978-1-4335-3516-1

Library of Congress Cataloging-in-Publication Data

Name: Schuchardt, Read Mercer, author.
Title: Media, journalism, and communication: a student's guide / Read Mercer Schuchardt.
Description: Wheaton, Illinois : Crossway, [2018] | Series: Reclaiming the Christian intellectual tradition | Includes bibliographical references and index.
Identifiers: LCCN 2017031568 (print) | LCCN 2017046808 (ebook) | ISBN 9781433535154 (pdf) | ISBN 9781433535161 (mobi) | ISBN 9781433535178 (epub) | ISBN 9781433535147 (tp) | ISBN 9781433535178 (ePub) | ISBN 9781433535161 (Mobipocket)
Subjects: LCSH: Communication—Religious aspects—Christianity. | Mass media—Religious aspects—Christianity. | Communication—Study and teaching (Higher) | Mass media—Study and teaching (Higher) | Learning and scholarship—Religious aspects—Christianity. | Education, Higher—Religious aspects—Christianity.
Classification: LCC P94 (ebook) | LCC P94 .S38 2018 (print) | DDC 302.23071/1—dc23
LC record available at https://lccn.loc.gov/2017031568

Crossway is a publishing ministry of Good News Publishers.

VP		28	27	26	25	24	23	22	21	20	19	18
15	14	13	12	11	10	9	8	7	6	5	4	3	2	1

To my students

CONTENTS

SERIES PREFACE

RECLAIMING THE CHRISTIAN INTELLECTUAL TRADITION

The Reclaiming the Christian Intellectual Tradition series is designed to provide an overview of the distinctive way the church has read the Bible, formulated doctrine, provided education, and engaged the culture. The contributors to this series all agree that personal faith and genuine Christian piety are essential for the life of Christ followers and for the church. These contributors also believe that helping others recognize the importance of serious thinking about God, Scripture, and the world needs a renewed emphasis at this time in order that the truth claims of the Christian faith can be passed along from one generation to the next. The study guides in this series will enable believers to see afresh how the Christian faith shapes how we live, how we think, how we write books, how we govern society, and how we relate to one another in our churches and social structures. The richness of the Christian intellectual tradition provides guidance for the complex challenges that believers face in this world.

This series is particularly designed for Christian students and others associated with college and university campuses, including faculty, staff, trustees, and other various constituents. The contributors to the series will explore how the Bible has been interpreted in the history of the church, as well as how theology has been formulated. They will ask: How does the Christian faith influence our understanding of culture, literature, philosophy, government, beauty, art, or work? How does the Christian intellectual tradition help us understand truth? How does the Christian intellectual tradition shape our approach to education? We believe that this series is not only timely but that it meets an important need, because the

11

secular culture in which we now find ourselves is, at best, indifferent to the Christian faith, and the Christian world—at least in its more popular forms—tends to be confused about the beliefs, heritage, and tradition associated with the Christian faith.

At the heart of this work is the challenge to prepare a generation of Christians to think Christianly, to engage the academy and the culture, and to serve church and society. We believe that both the breadth and the depth of the Christian intellectual tradition need to be reclaimed, revitalized, renewed, and revived for us to carry this work forward. These study guides will seek to provide a framework to help introduce students to the great tradition of Christian thinking, seeking to highlight its importance for understanding the world, its significance for serving both church and society, and its application for Christian thinking and learning. The series is a starting point for exploring important ideas and issues such as truth, meaning, beauty, and justice.

We trust that the series will help introduce readers to the apostles, church fathers, Reformers, philosophers, theologians, historians, and a wide variety of other significant thinkers. In addition to well-known leaders such as Clement, Origen, Augustine, Thomas Aquinas, Martin Luther, and Jonathan Edwards, readers will be pointed to William Wilberforce, G. K. Chesterton, T. S. Eliot, Dorothy Sayers, C. S. Lewis, Johann Sebastian Bach, Isaac Newton, Johannes Kepler, George Washington Carver, Elizabeth Fox-Genovese, Michael Polanyi, Henry Luke Orombi, and many others. In doing so, we hope to introduce those who throughout history have demonstrated that it is indeed possible to be serious about the life of the mind while simultaneously being deeply committed Christians.

These efforts to strengthen serious Christian thinking and scholarship will not be limited to the study of theology, scriptural interpretation, or philosophy, even though these areas provide the framework for understanding the Christian faith for all other areas of exploration. In order for us to reclaim and advance the Christian intellectual tradition, we must have some understanding of the tradition itself. The volumes in this series seek to explore this tradition and its application for our twenty-first-century world. Each volume contains a glossary, study questions, and a list of resources for further study, which we trust will provide helpful guidance for our readers.

I am deeply grateful to the series editorial committee: Timothy George, John Woodbridge, Michael Wilkins, Niel Nielson, Philip Ryken, and Hunter Baker. Each of these colleagues joins me in thanking our various contributors for their fine work. We all express our appreciation to Justin Taylor, Jill Carter, Allan Fisher, Lane Dennis, and the Crossway team for their enthusiastic support for the project. We offer the project with the hope that students will be helped, faculty and Christian leaders will be encouraged, institutions will be strengthened, churches will be built up, and, ultimately, that God will be glorified.

Soli Deo Gloria
David S. Dockery
Series Editor

INTRODUCTION:
ON PEDAGOGICAL ELEGANCE

Today's student needs to have an encyclopedic knowledge of everything in order to be able to do anything.

Marshall McLuhan

There is neither Jew nor Gentile, neither slave nor free, nor is there male and female, for you are all one in Christ Jesus.

Galatians 3:28 (NIV)

Media—Plural of *medium*, that which goes between. Any man-made object, tool, or process. Media are comprised of technologies, which are specific technical means for achieving specific technical ends.

Communication—The art of making many one. A form of rhetoric from a sender that attempts to persuade the receiver of a given relationship between the symbol and the symbolized.

Journalism—The daily news, so called because the time needed for production of the physical newspaper was one day, making today's newspaper yesterday's news. In digital culture, this is the newsfeed, updated by the minute and often initially reported before the event itself is over.

Look in your college viewbook or website, and somewhere you'll find one of the ultimate goals of your institution: *to turn you into a lifelong learner.* Your school says this, like most schools do, because it is indeed a noble and worthy aspiration. The only problem is that your school, like most schools these days, has no real idea how to achieve it.

But the ancient world did have a program. Around five hundred years before Christ, and fifty years before Malachi wrote his last prophetic words, the ancient Greeks devised a system that would guarantee the student, regardless of grade-point average, to become a lifelong learner. They understood that in order to teach the student the maximum number of individual-to-particular relations using the fewest number of subject areas, they would have to create a system that was cumulative, integrative, and irreducibly complex. In what later evolved into today's modern university, their system stood for centuries as the one best way to impart the knowledge of unity in all the diversity of the world around them.

This system, of course, was the original liberal arts. The liberal arts (Latin: *artes liberales*) were those subjects worthy and essential for a free person to know in order to participate in civic life, such as debating in public, defending yourself in court, serving on a jury, and doing your military service. Liberal arts didn't just mean *free*; it also meant the opposite of the servile arts (Latin: *artes vulgares*). If you were free, you studied these particular subjects to understand the entire cosmos and increase your wonder at the beauty, goodness, and intricacy of the created world. If you were not free, then you were a slave, and you studied the servile arts in order to better serve your masters. The world was divided into the power relationship of master or slave, and if you wanted to maintain your freedom, it behooved you to study well. And being "free" to study well presumed that you had the free time necessary to pursue the life of the mind precisely because you had slaves (or servants) to do the cooking, cleaning, and household and agricultural chores necessary to keep things running. The life of the mind was a much more expensive proposition back before robotic vacuum cleaners.

The seven liberal arts were made up of the *trivium* and the *quadrivium*. In many ways this was a perfect separation of form and content, or we might say it constituted a complete curriculum satisfying the needs of both the right and left hemispheres of the brain.

The trivium consisted of the three language-based studies: grammar, logic, and rhetoric. You can think of these at the simplest level: letters, words, sentences. They were, to be sure, much more than this. But you attend grammar school to learn your basics, you attend middle school to think clearly and logically, and you attend high school and college in order to master the art of persuasion, or rhetoric. You can't move on to the next level until you graduate from the previous one.

But the trivium was anything but trivial. It was cumulative, integrative, and irreducibly complex. It was also, if you look closely, an attempt to get learners to focus on the good, the true, and the beautiful: Grammar was the key to good sentences. Logic was the key to finding the truth of a situation. Rhetoric was the key to making beautiful speeches, and by extension, beautiful things (from Parthenons to democratic systems to political citizens). You couldn't do the next thing until you had mastered the previous thing. And you couldn't do the last thing if you forgot the first things. (This is why you are encouraged to "spell-check" your papers before turning them in.) But the key thing to notice is that, being language-based, the trivium was historically contingent, and therefore the subject of study would depend entirely upon where and when you happened to be born. To study the trivium in ancient Greece was not the same as studying the trivium in nineteenth-century Germany, which is not the same as studying it today in post-postmodern America: *Know w'am sayin'*?

But if language taught you the idiom and metaphor of your culture, and how to communicate in formal and informal settings, then you still needed the quadrivium to fill in the blanks, or the "what" of things. For this you would study the four subjects of math, geometry, music, and astronomy. To today's student with fifty or more majors to choose from, this old list of four typically looks like a random collection of "things the ancients thought worthy" but not much more. In truth, these four subjects, in this particular order, were the true genius of the system. The quadrivium, you see, is comprised entirely of number-based subjects of study. God, in his wisdom, made one world, and it is comprehensible to us to the degree that it is manifested in the universal and unwavering language of objectivity, or numbers. As such, the quadrivium represented a plan of study that was profoundly intelligent:

Math—the study of number
Geometry—the study of number in space
Music—the study of number in time
Astronomy—the study of number in motion (in space
    and time)

This project, like the trivium, was cumulative, integrative, and irreducibly complex. But it was also something more: it took the student from inside his head to placing his head into the cosmos itself. Math is the study of pure abstractions, which are merely concepts in one's head. In reality, there is no such thing as a "number," only the concept of number. So these calculations, performed in your head, can be performed using objects in the real world, but by and large to understand it, you need to be able to perform these calculations instantly, wordlessly, and accurately. Then, when the student studies geometry, he is suddenly able to leave the acoustic realm of concept and enter the visual realm of percept. In a point, a line, a surface, or a volume you suddenly "see" numbers in a way you never could before when they remained pure concept.

The word *geometry* actually meant "the measure of the earth," which will come up again later in the study of the planets, or "spheres" as the ancients called them. And for the ancients, this study of geometry was intimately connected with the growth of biological life itself. It could be called *a point, a line, a surface*, or *a volume*, or it could be called what was observed in nature's growth cycle: *a seed, a stem, a leaf*, or *a fruit*. The perceptual observation of nature confirmed the objective truth of geometry: clearly there was a pattern here that was intended by the Designer.

And then the student picked up his violin. Or lyre. Or harp. Or drums. And while musical instruments vary from culture to culture, and one would not play the same instrument in ancient Rome as in modern Japan, the fundamental thing is the same everywhere: organizing noises by keeping them in time. Music is "the study of number in time" because without the backbone of a consistent tempo, there simply is no music. In 1662, Thomas Fuller wrote that "music is nothing else but wild sounds civilized into time and tune."[1] Even an experimental musician like John Cage is demonstrating this when he goes against convention and makes musical exceptions that prove the rule. You may attend the concert, but you wouldn't put that stuff on your iPod. Why? Because you can't dance to it; it has no rhythm. But music is also much more than just the study of number in time. Music is how a student would incorporate the truth of numbers into his very body; it is where he first learned to re-incarnate the concept as percept. And in harmony with other musicians, it was an allegory of how he would learn to be part of the body politic.

For example, the conductor stops the music if just one player is off beat. And then you start again. And then when everybody gets it, the music soars and you feel yourself a member of something in which the whole is greater than the sum of the individual parts. You intuitively recognize that you need the other people in society in order to make this beautiful music. And they need you. In biblical terms, this is what is meant by everyone being a different part of the body, but all of them being important (1 Cor. 12:12–27).

So far, the ancient liberal arts program has taught the student how to communicate in his mother tongue, how to think concretely and abstractly, how to correlate concept with percept through geometry, how to incorporate these concepts and percepts into his

---

[1] Thomas Fuller, *The History of the Worthies of England* (1662).

body with music, how to be a part of a whole with other musicians, and now he is ready for the final study: astronomy.

Astronomy is the study of number in motion. And this motion takes place in space and time because the planets are actually in space and their movements can be measured in time—in fact, how long they take to move is the very essence of what defines time as we know it. The length of one year is 365 days, but that is just the amount of time it takes for the planets to revolve around each other, from our point of view. To understand how they worked was to peer into the very mind of the maker and see how the designer (gods and goddesses to the ancients, God to the monotheists) designed the entire system. Astronomy was also called "the music of the spheres." By this the ancients meant that the way the planets were arranged in mathematical order revealed the grand mastery, or musicianship, of the designer.

It is also worth noting that the seven liberal arts coincided with the seven ancient planets, the seven musical notes, the seven muses, and numerous other groups of seven. In AD 27, the Romans built the Pantheon, the temple for "all the gods" (by which they meant seven): from the ancient world up through the Middle Ages, the symbolic value of these correspondences was inseparable from the high degree of psychological reassurance the average citizen had in knowing that the world made sense. And these seven studies were all precedent to the ultimate study—theology—in which the student could approximate an understanding of the very mind of God by taking the first seven studies seriously.

In some sense, we might even say that the quadrivium constituted the objective truth of reality, one reason why theology was called "the queen of the sciences" up through the medieval period. God, if he were to be taken seriously, must have spoken objectively, clearly, and universally in his creation: he must therefore have "spoken" in the objective language of numbers and math. So by studying the four number-based studies of the quadrivium, you would be more and more qualified to perceive how it all fit together. It was only later in the seventeenth century and beyond that theology was demoted to one of the lower-paid levels of the humanities, where it ultimately became a subset of rhetorical interpretation.

The quadrivium, being number based, was therefore relatively ahistorical and noncontingent upon cultural factors such as the time and place of birth in history. So while studying the trivium in ancient Greece would be very different from studying the trivium in medieval England, the study of math and geometry would be largely the same. While musical instrumentation and styles changed throughout history, the student was still, always and everywhere, studying how to keep the beat, to keep number in time, using his body (fingers and/or mouth) on either a stringed or wind instrument of some sort, unless he was the drummer, in which case he used all of his body and was the very backbone of the band.

Whether you currently value these seven subject areas or not, you should nevertheless be able to see the nature and pedagogical elegance of the ancient program. How can we transmit to the young a sense of unity in the great diversity that we find in the cosmos? How can we give them a golden thread that will hold it all together in their understanding? And how can we do this using the smallest number of subject areas so as to minimally burden their young and developing minds? And finally, how can we do this in such a way that it produces that most desirable of effects, the creation of lifelong learners?

The answer to all these questions was the cumulative, integrative, progressive, and irreducibly complex nature of the seven liberal arts, and for around twenty centuries, it did truly fulfill the meaning of the term *elegance*: maximal structural integrity using minimal material means. The ancients' pedagogical elegance was just this because it gave the student the highest understanding of everything using the smallest number of anything; it gave them the greatest number of universals using the least number of particulars.

The reason it produced the effect of becoming a lifelong learner was that it taught the secret of the universe: that nothing is outside the scope of the interconnectedness of all things. And if nothing was irrelevant, then nothing was boring. If you had a liberal arts education, then by studying just seven subjects you were now suddenly interested in all of them. You went to graduate school. You became a student of life. You didn't care about grades, you cared about knowledge. And along the way, you became useful to society rather than being another glazed-over Internet zombie, or what comedian Louis C. K. calls a "noncontributing zero."

In fact, there was only one problem with the ancient liberal arts system, and it was that it reduced the world to the master-slave dialectic alluded to earlier. For reasons beyond an individual's control, one was either among the in-crowd or the out-crowd, among the few or the many, free or slave. And it was into this Greco-Roman world that a new teacher, a Jewish rabbi from Palestine, came and showed an even more elegant way.

It is worth noting that Jesus began his life's work as a servile artist (a carpenter) and ended the last three years of his life as a liberal artist (a rabbi, or teacher). Yet central to his teaching was the idea that a slave of Christ was the truly free man, because Christ's followers did not define their freedom in exclusively political or economic terms. It was for this reason that the New Testament could admonish slaves to obey their masters, yet also encourage them to gain their political or economic freedom if possible. Paul's point about being able to sing while imprisoned and in chains was precisely this interior freedom that Christ alone was able to grant: it yielded a psychic freedom for the bearer that neither economic structure nor political fate could remove. This was a radically new definition of freedom that allowed its bearer to despise the world while simultaneously sympathizing with its self-induced plight. Thus there was no contradiction between a Christian who was persecuted for Christ's sake and a Christian who was also called to care for the orphan, the widow, and the poor (James 1:27). To be "poor in spirit" did not mean to be without resources; it simply meant that one's resources were not measured in exclusively economic terms (Matt. 5:3). In today's job market this is called *psychic compensation*, and it is the personal or subjective benefits you get from a job that are not measurable by its objective or financial benefits.

The world has not forgotten about Jesus Christ since he came two thousand years ago, but it has forgotten how and why his teaching represented such a radical shift from the old way of thinking. Jesus's teaching was in a certain sense a subversive activity in that it destroyed the old pedagogy's false dichotomy of either/or and created a new world of both/and. We shall see how shortly.

According to some scholars, Jesus likely did have a classical liberal arts education in the Pythagorean mathematical progression. Whether that can be known or not, what we do know for certain is that early on, from at least the age of twelve, he had an astonishing rhetorical faculty that impressed even the scribes and teachers of the Jerusalem temple (Luke 2:41–52). We also know that, as an adult, he never quite fit into the established educational, cultural, or religious metaphor of his day. He could persuade soldiers, fishermen, prostitutes, and tax collectors, but the one group of people he absolutely could not work with was the professionally religious. They were the ones who received his wrath when turning over the temple tables, and they were the ones he called "whitewashed tombs"—pretty on the outside, but inside, full of dead bones (Matt. 23:27). In fact, the scribes and Pharisees were so upset by Jesus's new teachings that they repeatedly plotted for, and ultimately called for, his crucifixion.

In pedagogical terms, the effect of Christ's teaching was not fully perceived until perhaps Paul wrote his letter to the Galatians, a far-flung network of first-century believers residing in ancient Turkey. It was in that letter that Paul first pointed out that Christ had demolished the old master-slave dialectic. This dichotomy was not a new insight of Hegel or Marx; it was as old as antiquity. What Christ showed us was that your status as master or slave in your culture's political economy *was not the ultimate identifier of the self*. Paul put it shockingly blunt: if you were one in Christ, then there was no longer any spiritual validity to the distinction between male and female, between Greek and Jew, or between master and slave (Gal. 3:28). While most would read this to mean that, in Christ, you were as culturally validated as a *Greek male master*, what it actually meant was just the opposite. It meant that you could choose only one enslavement: either to the world and its false dichotomies, or to Christ and his transcendence of the whole thing. Thus, under the new assumption, you could actually have the political and economic status of a *Jewish female slave* and yet, paradoxically, be as completely "free" as the Greek male master. Given the burden and temptations of wealth (cf. Matt. 19:24), Christ's teachings suggested that the Jewish female slave could actually be freer than the Greek male master, because economic and political power were their own form of slavery. One might be a physical slave but if metaphysically free, then one could be imprisoned and find oneself singing, as Paul himself demonstrated (cf. Acts 16:16–40). And yet slavery was a pretty miserable circumstance, and Scripture never made light of it—in fact, Scripture made clear that, if possible, one should work to attain political and economic freedom (1 Cor. 7:21). If that were impossible, however, the Christian need not worry that this was the ultimate bondage. The language of the New Testament is rife with the joy of becoming a slave to Christ, suggesting that metaphysical slavery might yield the ultimate human freedom.

Today, of course, we've lost most of the pattern recognition that the ancients had, and we are faced with an overwhelming daily deluge of new and contradictory information, making it a full-time job just to keep up with what's happening, let alone understand it.

Today we attend liberal arts colleges and universities without the slightest clue of what the words mean—we just know we're supposed to do it. As a result, today's digital students are in a situation remarkably similar to that of the ancient world, except that their option to be free or slave is now largely derived by a combination of choice, fate, and diligence.

Upon graduation from a Christian liberal arts college, a graduate is just as likely to be a Starbucks barista as to be a Wall Street intern. He or she will as likely become a servile artist as a liberal artist and will do so both because the political economy of contemporary culture requires it, but also because Christ justifies all work (physical or mental) as equally worthy and redeemable. To prepare our students for this world is to remember Christ's indifference to vocational calling of free or slave, of liberal or servile artist. Common sense (not to mention their parents) will continually remind them which one is preferable, and necessity (not to mention student loans) will largely make the choice for them.

Today's college student feels the weight of the educational *blivet bag*—where you try to squeeze ten pounds of stuff into a five-pound sack—and as a result, experiences college mostly as a quixotic[2] exercise in frustration. Added to this, many liberal arts colleges are still using nineteenth-century media and pedagogical assumptions to prepare students for the twenty-first-century world. Thus, what contemporary Christian educators need to reflect profoundly on as they restructure their curricula is precisely this core question of elegance: How can we give students the minimal amount of content to produce the maximal result in personal freedom over the choices they make with the educational and vocational resources at their disposal? How can we provide a liberal arts education with Christ at the core that actually liberates our students to a vocational calling of—should they choose it—a servile art?

---

[2] *Quixotic*; adj., ideal but impractical.

Studying media, journalism, and the communication arts can be a liberating mode of *interdisciplinary simplexity*—a satisfying way of trying to learn everything you'll need to know before embarking on any successful career in anything, including graduate school. Interdisciplinary simplexity offers three things that are not currently available in most classrooms. First, simplexity takes the student beyond the simplicity-to-complexity (i.e., grade school-to-college) evolution by elevating discourse at increasingly accessible levels of communication. Second, simplexity promises availability of abundant content to the interested user while simultaneously not compromising maintenance of the overall picture. Third, simplexity allows the user to maintain coherence amid a perpetually overwhelming information environment by receiving information in smaller and easier-to-digest units.

Simplexity is explanatory of the paradoxical facts that (1) a weekday edition of the *New York Times* contains more information than the average person was likely to come across in a lifetime in seventeenth-century England as well as the fact that (2) many of today's newspapers are written at the fifth- to eighth-grade reading level. Simplexity, by the way, is where today's student already is: one reason why students spend so much time reading 140-character tweets and watching seven-second vines. The more information there is, the more they will need it to be byte-sized. By studying media, journalism, and the communication arts, the student is given a way of studying the forms of human communication throughout history, and along the way, acquiring a substantive portion of the content of those forms at no extra charge.

So how can you study history, war, economics, psychology, business, education, and religion all at once? By studying the changing nature of media forms, which have all, in each and every case, redefined the meaning of history, war, economics, psychology, business, education, and religion along the way.

Under conditions of information overload, interdisciplinary

simplexity is the only pattern possible for students to recognize, precisely because pattern recognition is the only form of intellectual taxonomy available at the speed of light. With a daily diet of 12 hours of media ingestion as their average, today's students are largely forced to improvise their ways through school. But that improvisation, like a jazz musician, is capable of producing great insight if it's pulling its cords and riffing off of such a rich media diet. We just need to remind students, on a daily basis, to not be so biased toward electronic or digital media only. We still need to teach them how to read.

To misremember the elegance of the ancient liberal arts and Christ's original revision of that curriculum is to misguide our students into any possible freedom they might have in an otherwise totalizing and technologically determined society. We must prepare them for the present world, not for an imagined future of a replayed past.

AND THIS, OF COURSE, IS *WHY YOU SHOULD MAJOR IN COMMUNICATION*

The one-stop-shopping phenomenon is nowadays contained in what's called Big Box Retail stores. Places like Walmart and Target are huge architectural boxes in the middle of suburban parking lots that allow you to get your food, replace your car battery, and buy a new dress all at once. You can also buy furniture, computers, toys, and a branded hot beverage, doughnut, or both. Instead of driving all over town to ten different places, you can get all your daily needs met with one stop, and there's a 5 percent "rewards card" to incentivize you to do just that.

In the modern educational system, this is called the communication major. Some call it the communication*s* major, but either way, it is the one-stop equivalent and best effort that schools today have of transmitting to you the "everything" they need to teach you in order to become a lifelong learner. It is the closest thing modern universities and colleges have to a system of "pedagogical elegance" that also teaches you the value and need of lifelong learning. You know that the current software is going to be obsolete by the time you graduate, so you have to keep up with the latest patches, downloads, and updates in order to stay current. You know that to work well in sound, you can't just "plug stuff in" but you actually need to know the science and mechanics and physics of both the sound booth and the inner ear. You know, from bitter experience, what a feedback loop is in both theory and practice, as proven by the buzzing and jarring acoustic assault that happened last time you placed the microphone too close to the amplifier.

Communication, media arts, and journalism are all essentially the latest evolutionary form of English departments, which are themselves outgrowths of the ancient grammar-logic-rhetoric track—which was itself the most important side or "half" of the *artes liberales*. Grammar was not just a lesson in "reading"—it was at root an allegorical exegesis of nature's phenomena, and it taught us how to "read" beneath the surface of things to recognize deeper patterns, using language as our observational tool set.

Nowadays most communication majors comprise both a theory and a practice track, so you can both mentally prepare your understanding of the field and also practice your hands-on, working knowledge of the latest technological tools. So under *theory* you might take a history of mass media or a communication theory course. Under the *practice* wing you might take public speaking, or journalism, or nonlinear video editing. And even though the curriculum or professors aren't telling you this, you are acquiring ancient and valuable skills: Interpersonal communication really will help you to be a better citizen. Public speaking really does often teach you how to beat a traffic ticket and thereby represent yourself in court, or join a public debate, or simply speak up for your neighbors at a town-hall meeting. And your student loans will often enough incentivize you (or your friends) to perform your military duty. So even though it's not nearly as systematic, clear, intuitive, or obvious, the communication major really is the one that more and more students are choosing for a host of reasons.

Cicero used to tell his rhetoric students that the orator needed to know everything that could be known; today, the one best way of attempting that impossible task (impossible, by the way, only since around 1800, thanks to the information explosion produced by the printing press and subsequent media technologies[3]) is to major in communication. It's the best major for telling you "everything about everything" because it incorporates history, science, language, psychology, philosophy, business, economics, theology, biology, chemistry, and many of the other majors. James Gleick's thesis in his book *The Information* is that what we've actually discovered after six thousand years of human history is that ALL of life is understandable as a "communication theory," whether it be communication between people, machines, cells, or atoms. Practically speaking, one of the biggest reasons for the growth of the communication arts major is simply the value of post-college employment: surveys tell us that among the top ten skill sets employers are looking for, "communication skills" are always at the top of the list. And this doesn't just mean that you should be a good, clear, personable, gregarious communicator; it also means you should be able to help your employer understand and function in the new world of a million apps and 34 gigabytes of daily information per person per day. Social media networking abilities such as Facebook, Twitter, Instagram, and Snapchat are all employable skills. And if you are really good at these things, you can go and work at those companies themselves.

So that's the theory. For the rest of this book, we'll discuss the ways in which the media is everything, the ways in which the media is lying to you, the ways in which the media is an alternative

---

[3] See, for example, Andrew Robinson's book about Thomas Young (1773–1829) titled *The Last Man Who Knew Everything* (St. Paul, MN: Pioneer Press, 2006), 179.

or substitute form of religion, and the ways in which the media is harder to see, perceive, and understand than ever before, and what you can do about it in order to become useful to yourself and your culture by becoming a user of the media rather than becoming used by the media.

1

WHY MEDIA MATTERS MORE NOW THAN EVER BEFORE

In the first place, we should clarify and define the basic terms under discussion. The word *media* is plural of the word *medium*, and that word simply means "that which goes between"—which is why the word is used to describe everything from how you like your steak cooked to your t-shirt size to a spiritual guide who contacts the dead. But the irony is that we use the word *media* in its singular form almost all the time, and almost always unconsciously.

Right now in America there are 1,780 commercial television stations,[1] 15,503 broadcast radio stations,[2] 1,331 newspapers,[3] 2,000,000 billboards,[4] and 5,821 movie theaters.[5] Worldwide there are over 7 billion cell phone subscriptions (comprising 4.77 million mobile phone users,[6] many of whom have more than one phone)

---

[1] "Number of Commercial TV Stations in the United States from 1950 to 2016," Statista website, May 2017, https://www.statista.com/statistics/189655/number-of-commercial-television-stations-in-the-us-since-1950/.

[2] Federal Communications Commission, "Broadcast Station Totals as of September 30, 2017," *News*, October 2, 2017, http://transition.fcc.gov/Daily_Releases/Daily_Business/2017/db1002/DOC-346998A1.pdf.

[3] "Number of Daily Newspapers in the United States from 1985 to 2014," Statista website, March 2015, https://www.statista.com/statistics/183408/number-of-us-daily-newspapers-since-1975/.

[4] Penneco Outdoor Advertising, "23 Astonishing Billboard Statistics You Must See to Believe," Penneco website, November 3, 2016, http://pennecooutdoor.com/billboard-statistics/.

[5] "Number of Cinema Sites in the United States from 1995 to 2016," Statista website, January 2017, https://www.statista.com/statistics/188643/number-of-us-cinema-sites-since-1995/.

[6] "Number of Mobile Phone Users Worldwide from 2013 to 2019 (in Billions)," Statista website, August 2015, https://www.statista.com/statistics/274774/forecast-of-mobile-phone-users-worldwide/.

and 1,276,011,353 million websites,[7] and this information became obsolete between the time these sentences were written and the time this book went to print because by the time you read this, there will be more of all the above (except for hardcopy print newspapers, which are dying like flies). But why do we say "the media" instead of "the medium" when discussing any or all of it? I think the answer, or at least part of the answer, lies in the facts that: (1) we don't know the source of our information, and (2) we experience media as a singular thing.

It's like the news—which used to be something that you went to, picked up, turned on, read, watched, or listened to *actively* in order to be informed. Today, however, news has become the thing that happens when someone runs up to you and says, "OMG, did you hear . . . ?" In its effect, which is to say, in our psychological perception, the media is just something that is and something that happens. And because it happens all the time—continuously, indiscreetly, and without interruption—we experience it as a singular entity. The question, "Says who?" never comes to our mind or our lips, and we simply do the search engine query, find the hit, and click the link. If we see, read, or hear the story on the media, then it must be true. This of course is the opposite of the truth, and it is often a lie, but the ways in which the media lies to us is something we'll discuss in detail later.

The second term we have to define is *communication*. The official definition usually contains historical information about the message, sender, receiver, channel, feedback, and noise. The signal-to-noise ratio should be just right in order for good communication to occur. And in the days of the telegraph, that was certainly true. Today, under our perpetual high definition conditions, the digital camera can present us with higher resolution than traditional 35mm

---

[7] Of all the statistics claimed here, this one is the most fun to track, because the number changes by several hundred between the time you begin writing it down and the time you finish writing it. Thus, this number was reasonably accurate at 11:15 a.m. CST on Friday, October 27, 2017. "Total Number of Websites," Internet Live Stats website, http://www.internetlivestats.com/total-number-of-websites/.

cameras ever could. Most often we are presented with such high signal strength that it becomes its own form of noise, such as the way the new super high-definition TV shows and movies annoyed you at first (until you got used to them) because they were too "lifelike" and not "cinematic" enough. People said it was like watching a documentary, or worse, a live play, in their living room. But again, we live mythically now, and all our past processes are simply taken for granted, so the best way of defining communication is in its effect, not its cause.

Communication is the art of making many one. It requires the science of the technological tools that make it possible, but it is an art because sometimes it works, like *Star Wars*, and sometimes it doesn't, like *Avatar*—a film so successful that you can't name any characters except for "that one blue guy." It is ultimately an etymological definition, as it shares the same root as the words *community*, *communal*, and *communion*. Originally, it meant "to have something in common with someone else."

This desire for an effect of shared experience is why it is especially important for Christians to study communication. Scripture tells us clearly that Jesus, the Holy Spirit, and the future heaven on earth are all going to have this characteristic of shared common experience and perception. "Every knee shall bow to me, and every tongue shall confess to God" (Rom. 14:11) is another way of saying "to make many one." The lack of visual descriptors but prevalence of acoustic descriptors about heaven, in which men and women and angels and archangels are all singing before the Lord, is another way of saying "to make many one." Studies show that the quickest and most effective way to unify an otherwise disparate group into a cohesive unit is to get them to sing a song together. The word *unify* means "to make one." The word *unit* means "one."

The dream and goal and hope of Scripture is for all mankind to become one in Christ. To get there, we should learn to communicate better. To become one with Christ, we eat his body and drink his blood in the sacrament of communion. The book of Acts is a description of the amazing things that can happen—economic, social, political, psychological, spiritual—when this oneness occurs in a community. The word *communication* also shares the root meaning of *communism*, a failed political experiment in which the state takes the place of God as a nonvoluntary organizing and unifying force. The coercive nature of the project has proved its undoing in various countries, but the quixotic goal of unifying society under the barrel of a gun (through fear) continues to be attempted today. Through greed—which is the communist critique of a purely capitalist society—the effort is equally quixotic. But through the voluntary and free-will act of sacrificial love, which is Scripture's method, the project has shown fruitfulness at different times and places through history.

So why does the media matter now more than ever? Well, the blunt reality is that your parents, teachers, and religious leaders have been lying to you all along. They meant well, they intended the best, but they haven't ever told you the truth. And that's not because they didn't mean to, want to, or try to—they are good people, for the most part. But the lie they told you wasn't in the content of anything they said. The lie they told you was that they were your parents, your teachers, and your religious leaders. The truth is, they weren't. The media was, and is, and will be, until you die. Just look at the numbers:

Average hours an American child spends face to face with his
     parents each week: 14[8]
Average hours an American child spends face to face with his
     television each week: 35

Average hours an American child spends per week at school: 30
Average hours an American child spends per week with various
     digital screens: 77

---

[8] Brigid Schulte, "Making Time for Kids? Study Says Quality Trumps Quantity" *Washington Post*, March 28, 2015, https://www.washingtonpost.com/local/making-time-for-kids-study-says-quality-trumps-quantity/2015/03/28/10813192-d378–11e4–8fce–3941fc548f1c_story.html.

Average hours an American believer spends in religious services
per week: 3
Average hours an American believer spends in media time per
week: 84

Number of hours in a week: 168
Average hours Americans spend indoors each week: 146
Average hours Americans spend outdoors each week: 12
Average hours Americans spends in a car each week: 10[9]

Average sleeping hours in 1800 (before the industrial
revolution): 10
Average sleeping hours in 1850 (after industrial revolution): 9.5
Average sleeping hours in 1910 (after electricity and gas lights): 9
Average sleeping hours in 1972 (after mom went to work): 8
Average sleeping hours in 1997 (after the Internet): 7
Average sleeping hours in 2007 (after smartphones): 6.5[10]

This may come as slightly shocking or be completely obvious
to you, but we now receive our parenting, our pedagogical instruc-
tion, and our religious wisdom far more from the media than from
any other source, including parents, teachers, and religious leaders
combined. Obviously the above numbers are averages, and your
personal numbers may be higher or lower. It's worth taking the
time to do your own personal inventory and then try to quantify
just "how much" of your parenting is received from your parents,
how much of your teaching comes from your teachers, and how
much of your religion comes from religious leaders.

You might also find it instructional to run your own numbers to
discover whether or not media plays the role of default idolatry in your
life. Without being conscious of it, it's easy to see how the true and

[9] Neil Klepeis et al., "The National Human Activity Pattern Survey (NHAPS): A Resource for Assessing Exposure to Environmental Pollutants," *Journal of Exposure Analysis & Environmental Epidemiology* 11 (February 6, 2001): 231–52, http://www.nature.com/jes/journal/v11/n3/full/7500165a
.html.
[10] "Annual Sleep in America Poll Exploring Connections with Communications Technology Use and
Sleep," National Sleep Foundation, March 7, 2011, https://sleepfoundation.org/media-center/press
-release/annual-sleep-america-poll-exploring-connections-communications-technology-use-and-sleep.

the living God could come out in second, third, or hundredth place in your life if you compare the numbers. Quantitatively, what the God of Scripture demands of us is pretty mild compared to what media demands from us. God simply wants one tenth of your money and one seventh of your time. The tithe and the Sabbath are two key ways of quantifying "what God wants" from you. If you consider these in the strictest and most literal sense, you find some pretty shocking results.

TITHE

The average American tithes 2.5 percent of his income. If the average individual income is $26,000 in 2016 and the average household income is $54,000, then this means the average American is giving between $650 ($12.50 per week) and $1,350 ($25.96 per week) to his church, when what God actually wants is between $2,600 and $5,400. In 2012, just five years after the iPhone was introduced, the total cost of ownership (device, service contract, surcharges, taxes, case, car charger, stereo dock, etc.) for an iPhone 5 was between $1,800 per year (for the 16GB model) and $4,800 per year (for the 64GB model). That's a "media tithe" between $34.61 and $92.30 per week, or roughly three times what American Christians give to their churches, and between 70 and 90 percent of what God actually requires. And that, of course, is just for the smartphone, whose average lifespan is two years.

When you run the same numbers for your computer and for your wall-sized, flat-panel LCD TV, you discover that most Americans that own all three devices are spending quite a bit more. For a member of the cult of Mac, here's a rough breakdown of what it would look like in the first quarter of 2016.[11]

13-inch MacBook Pro laptop computer	$1,300
iPhone 6S with 5.5 inch display (128GB)	$950
Sony 75-inch LCD flat-panel smart TV	$1,600
Hardware costs	$3,850

[11] Jaime Rivera, "The Total Cost of Ownership for an iPhone 5 Is $1,800," *PocketNow*, October 3, 2012, http://pocketnow.com/2012/10/03/the-total-for-an-iphone-5-is-1800.

Average cost of combined Internet/cable TV	$480
	($40 monthly)
Average cost of cell-phone subscription	$480
	($40 monthly)
Netflix standard plan per year	$120
Software costs (subscriptions) per year	$1,080
Total cost of smartphone ownership for two years (average lifespan)	$6,010
Total cost of smartphone ownership/membership per year	$3,005
Total cost of smartphone ownership/membership per month	$250
Tithe percentage this amount represents for $26K median American salary	11.5 percent
Tithe percentage this amount represents for $54K median American salary	5.5 percent

SABBATH

God wants one-seventh of your time. For most American Christians, this actually amounts to 2 hours on a Sunday morning. If you are "really religious," you might also go to a midweek service and a small group or Bible study at some point during the week, which would total roughly 6 hours of your week. But even if you follow the strict Old Testament definition of the Sabbath, the most the Sabbath can take up of your time is one 24-hour period, from sundown to sundown, each week.

When times are compared, our media consumption habits, in terms of hours spent, are far more holy to us than the Sabbath by any stretch.

A Bureau of Labor Statistics study showed that of our leisure activities, Americans spent 2.8 hours per day watching TV in 2014. In 2015, Nielsen reported that Americans spend nearly 5 hours per day watching TV, and these numbers didn't include Netflix viewing. BTIG Research claimed that the average Netflix viewer was watching

2 hours per day in 2015, suggesting that some Americans are actually watching 7 hours of filmed entertainment per day. The data is hard to sort and assess completely accurately under multimedia conditions when someone can watch both TV and Internet programming on a smartphone, tablet, TV, or any number of "third screen" or "fourth screen" technologies, but overall the big picture of time spent in media consumption looked like this as of October 2015:

Daily minutes spent online (laptop and desktop)	132
Daily minutes spent on mobile phones	174
Daily minutes spent on other connected devices	23
Daily minutes spent on TV	251
Daily minutes spent on radio	87
Daily minutes spent on newspapers (nondigital)	17
Daily minutes spent on magazines (nondigital)	13
Daily minutes spent on movies, books, and other media	24
TOTAL	720

(12 hours daily)[12]

These numbers are, of course, "daily averages" and not actual counts of how each of us spends our days. Taken from our weekly and monthly habits though, these numbers show what it would look like if we allotted media time evenly across each day.

As you can see from the chart, 12 hours per day is a full Sabbath's worth of time every two days. Thus, by the time Sunday actually rolls around, we have already spent three full days *without sleep* on media consumption. *Now that's devotion!* The word *worship* simply means "to ascribe worth to." And by paying this much

---

[12] Based on the following sources: "American Time Use Survey Summary," Bureau of Labor Statistics, US Department of Labor, June 24, 2016, http://www.bls.gov/news.release/atus.nr0.htm.

Demitrios Kalogeropoulos, "The Average American Watches This Much TV Every Day: How Do You Compare?" *The Motley Fool*, March 15, 2015, http://www.fool.com/investing/general/2015/03/15/the-average-american-watches-this-much-tv-every-day.aspx.

Lara O'Reilly, "Netflix Is Eating TV's Dinner: If It Were a TV Network It Would Be at Least the Fourth-Biggest in the US," *Business Insider*, April 16, 2015, http://www.businessinsider.com/average-daily-netflix-usage-according-to-btig-research--2015-4.

"Average Time Spent with Major Media per Day in the United States as of April 2017," Statista website, April 2016, http://www.statista.com/statistics/276683/media-use-in-the-us/.

attention to media, we are, by definition, ascribing worth to the experience. So if we take our hours of media consumption seriously, as a valid comparison and equivalency to time spent in worship, then what it means is that we've already gone to the church of our false idols about eighteen times in a week before we ever walk in the door of our real church.

But of course, it's not an entirely fair comparison because the nature of the media we use is not actually letting us decide the nature of the worth we are ascribing. Under digital technology conditions, all the barriers are broken, and everything is mixed up in everything else: there is no such thing as a "media for work" and "media for leisure" separation anymore. The cell phone that lets you be reached anywhere means, among other things, that you are always at work, or at least always "on call" to be responsive to any urgent work situation. And the corollary is also true: you are always "at home" even when you are at work, and able to receive calls to help manage any home crisis.

A recent study showed that 80 percent of college graduates would not take a job if it did not allow them to post social media updates during work hours. In other words, under digital media conditions, your life is your life is your life, and whether you're at work, at home, at play, or at church, you should be able to mediate it as much or as little as you want. So in that sense, it's a bit of a false dichotomy to say, "This media is for man," and "This media is for God." And if you go to a megachurch, it's even harder to know how/when/where to separate the wheat from the chaff. Are you being used by media? Are you using media? The answer is always yes, to both questions. What this little book hopes to do, by the end, is to make you a more conscious user, and a less susceptible usee.[13]

But suffice it to say, media is what we do now. In a world with 7.1 billion cell-phone subscriptions (over 2 billion of whom are smartphone users), we now live on a planet where media is the

---

[13] A good place to start is by googling the YouTube video "Contemporvant" (https://www.youtube.com/watch?v=giM04ESUiGw) to see a megachurch making fun of itself in November 2011 as it deploys emotionally manipulative techniques and technologies on its audience.

largest thing we all collectively do. When you look at sociological or demographic or psychographic markers of human behaviors, affinities, and consumption patterns, nothing else comes close:

> There are more cell-phone users than any one race or ethnicity has members.
>
> There are more cell-phone users than any one nation has members.
>
> There are more cell-phone users than any one language has members.
>
> There are more cell-phone users than any one religion has members.
>
> There are more cell-phone users than any one gender has members.
>
> There are more cell-phone users than any one sexual orientation has members.

Okay, that last one isn't yet true, but it will be very soon. If 3.5 percent of Americans are lesbian, gay, bisexual, or transgender (LGBT),[14] then it's fairly reasonable to predict that very soon the number of cell-phone users will be larger than the number of heterosexuals on planet earth. If the American number is accurate (a big *if*), and if that percentage is globally consistent (a much bigger *if*), then it means there are at least 250 million nonheterosexual persons on planet earth. By contrast, the only group (that I know of) that has a cultural prejudice against the use and ownership of cell phones is the Amish. The Amish exist only in America, and they are only 313,000 people,[15] or roughly the equivalent of 12 percent of the above estimated global LGBT population. As a percentage of the total global population, the Amish are a mere 0.004 per-

---

[14] This figure comes from a 2011 UCLA/Williams Institute study reported in Gary J. Gates, "How Many People Are Lesbian, Gay, Bisexual and Transgender?" The Williams Institute, UCLA School of Law, April 2011, http://williamsinstitute.law.ucla.edu/research/census-lgbt-demographics-studies/how-many-people-are-lesbian-gay-bisexual-and-transgender/. Numbers for the entire planet are harder to come by, thanks to a variety of factors, and figures range from 1.2 percent to 20 percent, depending on the study.

[15] "Amish Population Change, 1992–2017," Young Center for Anabaptist and Pietist Studies, Elizabethtown College, https://groups.etown.edu/amishstudies/files/2017/08/Population_Change_1992-2017.pdf.

cent of the human species. When indigenous Amazonian tribes are using cell phones,[16] you know it's time to consider it a truly global phenomenon.

If you don't think this is astonishing, consider that already there are more homeless people in America than there are people without televisions. And since 1998, there have been more drivable cars than licensed drivers in America. So the Internet-connected smartphone will most likely be the singular human technology that brings us all into the same technological "denomination" within the next ten years. For Christians, this fact should be worthy of serious consideration and reflection, especially since Scripture tells us that it is the name of Christ to which "every knee shall bow . . . and every tongue shall confess" (Rom. 14:11). Instead, it may turn out to be the name of Apple, or Samsung, or Nokia.

So this, in sum, is why media matters more today than ever before. In the past, media was something you picked up, used, and then put down to get on with your life. Now media is your life, or at least the way you access everything else necessary to get on with your life. If culture is the lens through which we perceive all of reality, then media is now that lens. There simply is no other single factor that dominates more of our time, attention, money, or interest. No matter what you major in, do for a living, believe or disbelieve in, you will be mediated.

But we weren't always mediated. How we got here is worth a few pages of your time.

THE GREAT CHAIN OF BEING

Things here on earth come in four types: matter, plants, animals, and humans. This is an ascending scale of significance in terms of function and capability.

---

[16] Adam Wernick, "In Brazil, Indigenous Tribes Are Still Struggling to Protect the Rainforest—and Their Culture," *Public Radio International*, March 10, 2014, http://www.pri.org/stories/2014-03-10/brazil-indigenous-tribes-are-still-struggling-protect-rainforest-and-their.

MATTER

[*Matter*]

The stuff rocks are made of and the various chemicals in the surrounding environment in various combinations. They are made up of matter. They are inert, but they are key ingredients in the other things that possess life.

PLANTS

[*Matter + Life*]

These are the variety of green and colorful things that are made of matter but that also have the seven characteristics of all biological life. These are (1) order, (2) sensitivity (responsiveness to stimuli), (3) reproduction, (4) growth and development, (5) regulation, (6) homeostasis, and (7) energy processing.

ANIMALS

[*Matter + Life + Consciousness*]

These are the variety of colorful or camouflaged organisms that don't stay where they are planted, but move about in the water, earth, or sky. They are made of matter and possess the characteristics of life, but also have a consciousness of themselves as organisms in an environment. This is why, when you call to your ficus tree, it does not answer. But when you call to your dog, it comes running.

HUMANS

[*Matter + Life + Consciousness + Consciousness of their consciousness*]

These are people like you. These organisms come in fairly standard shapes, of varying sizes and colors, and are made of matter, are alive, are conscious, and have the unique perceptual ability of being "doubly conscious," or "conscious of their consciousness." The Latin name for this species (*Homo sapiens sapiens*) means the "ape that thinks about its thinking." The various names for this organism's unique characteristic is intellect, will, or language, but they all pretty much mean the same thing: that only humans have this capacity for awareness of themselves as existing in time, with the capacity to create, and with the awareness of their own mortality—one reason why they invent religions. The opposable thumb, the language instinct, and other allegedly unique traits really do signify that humans are the only naked species that got dressed, the only species that builds nuclear bombs, and the only species that thinks an alternative reality is preferable to nature. Whereas a man ponders his mortality and his own death for years, a dog simply crawls under the porch and dies. As G. K. Chesterton put it,

> It is true that in the spring a young quadruped's fancy may lightly turn to thoughts of love, but no succession of springs has ever led it to turn however lightly to thoughts of literature. And in the same way, while it is true that a dog has dreams, while most other quadrupeds do not seem even to have that, we have waited a long time for the dog to develop his dreams into an elaborate system of religious ceremonial. We have waited so long that we have really ceased to expect it; and we no more look to see a dog apply his dreams to ecclesiastical construction than to see him examine his dreams by the rules of psychoanalysis.[17]

So even though there are over two hundred years' worth of arguments suggesting that humans and animals are not so different after all, every one of these arguments boils down to what Walker Percy calls a very small commonality in defiance of a very large difference.

Here is the basic history of the communication modes of the human species

1. **Orality** (talking and listening and naming and remembering)
   - Time period of dominance: then–3200 BC
   - By "then" we mean whenever you surmise human culture began, acquired language, and began talking.

---

[17] G. K. Chesterton, *The Everlasting Man* (New York: Image, 1955), 50–51.

2. **Writing** (scratching symbols into clay, later drawing them on wood, papyrus, vellum, paper, etc.)
- 3200 BC–AD 1440

3. **Printing** (machine-setting the symbols and mass-producing the product, the beginning of the assembly line and the mass production of uniform goods)
- 1440–1839
- While the Chinese did "invent" printing much earlier (between the third and sixth centuries, depending on who you ask), their invention was the "woodblock" printing of a single "page" at a time. Gutenberg's invention in Germany (between 1440 and 1450) was different because he created each letter as a separate piece of hot metal type, so that the entire page could be rearranged as needed prior to printing.

4. **Electronic** (Morse code to television: using the power of electricity to transmit symbols at light speed, separating the speed of transmission from the speed of transportation)
- 1839–2007
- While the telegraph wasn't invented until 1844, we use 1839 as the start date because that is the year that Faraday "harnessed" electricity and the year that photography was invented.

5. **Digital** (the web 2.0 and beyond: the Internet, the smartphone, social media, and the perpetually tuned-in self)
- 2007–present
- While ARPANET's Ray Tomlinson sent the first email in 1971, the first commercial email wasn't sent until December 1990, and the Internet did not become a mass medium in America until 1997. We place the start of "digital" communication at 2007 because that is the year that everyone was on Facebook, the year that Apple introduced the iPhone, and the ten-year mark by which it was clear that digital communication wasn't going away. This date is contentious in both directions; even now (summer 2017), there are only

3.9 billion[18] people on the Internet (suggesting that
the Internet itself is not yet a "global" mass medium),
even as there are 7.1 billion cell-phone subscriptions.

IT'S A LINEAR HISTORY, BUT A CIRCULAR EFFECT

The history of mass media is just like any other long, winding, and historical chart of progressive steps to the present moment. But the reason you should pay closer attention to media, and take it seriously, is because in understanding the past, you can actually quite easily predict the future.

Every human invention or technology is, in some sense, a "medium" because it serves as a "go-between" between man and his environment. As such, it "translates" or "metaphorizes" our experience for us. This was the key insight of Marshall McLuhan, quite possibly the best and brightest of all the media theorists you will ever study (and certainly, along with Neil Postman, the one who gets my highest ranking). So when you look at where we've come from and then try to speculate about where we are going, the matter becomes quite clear, quite quickly: the future is verbal. That is to say, in the very near future, all your technological media forms will be voice-recognized and voice-controlled. You will update Facebook verbally, rather than by keyboard and mouse. The skill of typing will become as rapidly obsolete as the skill of map reading in the age of GPS. In a way, this world is already here: you talk to Siri, you talk to your car, your car and your GPS talk to you. Amazon's Alexa-enabled Tap device allows you to ask it everything from weather reports to playing your favorite song. Voice-to-text and text-to-voice software technologies will soon make everyone's language, dialect, and idiolect completely "known" to the technologies they are interacting with on a daily basis. And this will be a return to the very first media stage, Orality. Walter Ong called

---

[18] Miniwatts Marketing Group, "Internet Users in the World by Regions," Internet World Stats website, June 30, 2017, http://www.internetworldstats.com/stats.htm.

it "Secondary Orality" in the electronic age, and we might term it "Tertiary Orality" under digital conditions, but whatever you call it, the results are the same.

Now as soon as you notice this, some interesting corollaries apply:

Txtng is the new Hbrw—No vowels are needed when you already know the context.

Emojis are the new hieroglyphics—The Israelites left Egypt and discovered their alphabet on the way to the Promised Land, most likely at Mt. Sinai. Today's student wants to convey a rich amount of emotional context to her texting, so she deploys single-button emoticons or emojis to convey the feeling or context around her otherwise-cryptically minimalist letters.

This produces our current communication pattern, in which we are: (a) moving away from full-length sentences and toward texting that is shorter, quicker, and easier; (b) enhancing our texting with more emojis; and (c) heading toward ever-greater complexity in the "content" of our emojis (think of the significance, when it first happened, of "skin-toned" emojis). Taken together, this reveals a reversal of the human communication history timeline. In other words, we are regressing to a more primitive, less abstract, less rational, and more emotional mode, style, and means of communicating. This has HUGE implications in all areas and is but one more reason why you should be studying media.

PRINT IS DEAD—LONG LIVE PRINT!

If you haven't heard, print is dead.[19] After a five-hundred-year reign in the Western world, the medium of print communication has pretty much outright died. The newspaper world is moving online, the book world is printing more and more books that no one is

---

[19] The best take on this tragedy is, in fact, comedy: "Print Dead at 1,803," *The Onion*, July 25, 2013, http://www.theonion.com/article/print-dead-at-1803-33244.

reading, and the state of literacy in the world is on the decline. The image has trumped the word, and the screen has defeated the page. The implications this has for the future of journalists, magazine writers, and book authors has yet to be fully recognized. But rather than lament the death of the previous dominant communication medium, it's much more helpful to understand its historical place, its cultural significance, and its likely future as a form of nostalgia. The book is the beard of the future. The tattoo parlor is tomorrow's printing press: your skin is the new vellum.

One of the biggest challenges, problems, headaches, and nightmares of today's colleges and universities is that they were born in the manuscript age, reached their peak in the print age, and now don't know what to do with themselves. The oldest university in the West is the University of Bologna, Italy, founded in 1088. By the time the Italian paper industry was going full swing, the need for a manufacturing system became so great that Gutenberg's printing press arrived just in time to save the backs, necks, and wrists of thousands of scribes. In fact, you might even say that the printing press produced the modern university as we know it: a place where books are created, stored, studied, read, and discussed by those with the leisure time to do so (the free ones, studying the *artes liberales*, remember?). Today, the university libraries are busy not expanding their shelves, but collapsing them in favor of digital editions, eBooks, and online subscriptions to databases once housed in bulky scholarly journals. As all information migrates online, the reason for going to the library has changed from "for the books" to other, less obvious reasons: for the free Wi-Fi, for the good coffee, for the chance of meeting someone new. The book as store of knowledge is giving way to the book as fashion accessory. Studies show that the average college graduate reads between zero and one book per year.[20]

---

[20] Lee Rainie and Andrew Perrin, "Slightly Fewer Americans Are Reading Print Books, New Survey Finds," October 19, 2015, Pew Research Center, http://www.pewresearch.org/fact-tank/2015/10/19/slightly-fewer-americans-are-reading-print-books-new-survey-finds/.

JOURNALISM 2.0: CORPORATE AND GOVERNMENT SPONSORSHIP VS. PROPAGANDA

There is no such a thing in America as an independent press, unless it is out in country towns. You are all slaves. You know it, and I know it. There is not one of you who dares to express an honest opinion. If you expressed it, you would know beforehand that it would never appear in print. I am paid $150 for keeping honest opinions out of the paper I am connected with. Others of you are paid similar salaries for doing similar things. If I should allow honest opinions to be printed in one issue of my paper, I would be like Othello before twenty-four hours: my occupation would be gone. The man who would be so foolish as to write honest opinions would be out on the street hunting for another job. The business of a New York journalist is to distort the truth, to lie outright, to pervert, to villify, to fawn at the feet of Mammon, and to sell his country and his race for his daily bread, or for what is about the same — his salary. You know this, and I know it; and what foolery to be toasting an "Independent Press"! We are the tools and vassals of rich men behind the scenes. We are jumping-jacks. They pull the string and we dance. Our time, our talents, our lives, our possibilities, are all the property of other men. We are intellectual prostitutes.[21]

It is not enough for journalists to see themselves as mere messengers without understanding the hidden agendas of the message and myths that surround it.[22]

Journalism at its best pursues the facts about certain situations in which evildoers are at work and assembles those facts and judges them fairly. It's not a crusade so much as it's a responsible gathering of a body of evidence that, when it's finally presented, is so persuasive that evil must skulk, retreat or be subjected to strong public remedy. . . . Why wouldn't Christian believers want to be part of that?[23]

---

[21] John Swinton, quoted in "John Swinton," Wikiquote website, September 22, 2015, https://en.wiki quote.org/wiki/John_Swinton.
[22] John Pilger, *Hidden Agendas* (Vintage, 1998), 4.
[23] John McCandlish Phillips, quoted in Terry Mattingly, "The Life and Times of John McCandlish Phillips," *On Religion* website, April 22, 2013, http://www.tmatt.net/columns/2013/04/the-life-and -times-of-john-mccandlish-phillips.

Under digital conditions, the newspaper has about the same chance at survival as the Dodo bird. It's all but over. Newspapers are dropping like flies. Every time a newspaper redesigns itself, its always to reduce the word count and increase the picture size. Gone is the editorial staff in favor of more graphic designers, photographers, and web-content managers. The *Chicago Tribune* laid off four hundred of its eight hundred in 2007, most of whom were on the editorial team. For the past ten years, newspapers have survived on the readership of baby boomers and the secondary uses the medium is good for: fire starters[24] and fish wrappers.[25] Even the old gimmick of putting in $20 worth of coupons into the $2.50 Sunday edition has failed to work in the days of smartphone-enabled electronic or web-based coupons.

The medium of print, in simple terms, is no longer sustainable. You have to kill trees to make newspapers, and that alone is evidence of environmental irresponsibility, right? Well, wrong, but it's a longer story than a simple equation of the "dead tree = unhealthy environment" argument. The reality is that trees are replantable and renewable, and most paper companies are economically incentivized to be environmentally friendly to their natural resources. The Internet, through which all information and journalism now flows, is actually the fifth-leading "country" in terms of electricity consumption (just behind China, the USA, Russia, and Japan, but ahead of India, Germany, Canada, and Brazil), using some 210 million megawatts per year.[26] Another study claims the Internet uses 10 percent of all electricity worldwide.[27] Whatever the actual number is, one thing is quite clear: the Internet is no friend

---

[24] I myself subscribe to the weekend-only print edition of the *Chicago Tribune* each fall in order to have enough paper for my fall and winter fires in the wood-burning stove that heats my home. I also read the paper before burning it, but not because I need to.

[25] One wonders if the decline of the late Catholic practice of "fish on Fridays" has itself contributed to the decline of newspaper subscribers in the past few decades?

[26] Katie Singer, "The Real Amount of Energy Used to Power the Internet," *An Electronic Silent Spring* (blog), January 28, 2015, http://www.electronicsilentspring.com/real-amount-energy-power -internet/.

[27] Tessel Renzenbrink, "How Much Electricity Does the Internet Use?" *Elecktor*, June 13, 2013, https://www.elektormagazine.com/articles/how-much-electricity-does-the-internet-use.

to the environment. Electricity production happens by coal, gas, nuclear, wind, or solar power, and in all of these methods there is a threat to the environment and the species that live within the area of production.

THE BAD NEWS

But bigger than the environmental threat posed by newspaper production is possibly the mental threat to the reader who is unaware of the source. According to *Harper's* magazine, three out of five newspaper stories are now press releases either from a government or a corporate agency. That's in a context where 50 to 65 percent of the paper is already taken up by advertising, with the leftover space referred to as "the news hole" that must be filled by editorial. So with at least half of a newspaper's content being advertising, and another 60 percent of the editorial content being market- or government-driven, it means the newspaper now (at best) contains roughly about 20 percent real "news" that is not driven by some corporate or state agenda.

Add to these threats the depressing state of global journalism, in which the journalist is now one of the most highly hazardous and life-threatening jobs available. It might seem exciting to become an international journalist covering foreign wars, but under digital conditions (i.e., Information Warfare conditions), just the reporting of your location can be interpreted as a hostile threat by either the enemy or by your own troops. The number of journalists killed in the line of duty grows with each passing year. According to the Committee to Protect Journalists,[28] between twenty-one and seventy journalists have been killed each year. Only 7 percent were on a dangerous assignment that resulted in death; 23 percent died in crossfire or combat situations, while a full 68 percent were murdered for motives related to their reporting.

---

[28] "1,218 Journalists Killed since 1992," Committee to Protect Journalists, accessed November 18, 2016, https://www.cpj.org/killed/.

This suggests the corporate and government press releases have a point to make, and provides one reason why "corporate journalism" and "embedded journalism" are the norms of the day. Corporate or brand journalism is very similar to public relations in effect, if not in cause. A corporate journalist is a real journalist, trained in research, writing, and editing like any other journalist, but whose work is put to use for the benefit of either a specific brand or a conglomeration of corporate interests. Embedded journalists are reporters attached to military units actively involved in armed conflicts, and they have come to the foreground in US military reporting since the second invasion of Iraq in 2003. The strengths of embedded journalism are that it provides better physical support and safety for the journalist, but doing so also restricts both where the journalist can go to get a story and who he can talk to to find a good story.

In both cases, critics of corporate and embedded journalism suggest that the story is always written before the journalist goes into the field: the angle of the story will always, by definition, favor the perception of the corporation or the government as the "good guys." In the simple dichotomy of *puff piece* or *takedown*, corporate or embedded journalists primarily write puff pieces for their employers or protectors. Thus, the world (as perceived through the news media) begins to sound more and more like an advertisement, which is more and more like propaganda. And under these conditions, the "news hole" can quickly turn into what George Orwell called the "memory hole" in his novel *1984*, in which today's truth is tomorrow's lie, and the public capacity for memory is overwhelmed by the flood of constantly new information. One of the unintentionally darkly humorous headlines of the past decade is the now-ubiquitous "Fresh Violence" that you see anywhere, at any time, as though it were equivalent to the fresh vegetables you can find at the market.

THE GOOD NEWS

The good news is that there is more news than ever. The *New York Times* website publishes about 250 articles a day. But the *Huffington Post* publishes 500 per day, and Yahoo over 3,000.[29] The only downside of this massive increase in news is that you can't read all that (a) because there aren't enough hours in the day, and (b) because online the ratio of press-release-masquerading-as-news to real news is likely to be equally high. The level of information overload that we are now subject to is literally unprecedented in history. According to one scholar, the average weekday edition of the *New York Times* contains more information than the average seventeenth-century English person would come across in his entire lifetime.[30] No wonder attention-deficit disorder (ADD) is a growth industry.

The other good news is that the truth is out there. It's just that now you have to be willing to dig and dig for it like a small, pointy, metal thing in a pile of agricultural feed straw. The key to finding needles in haystacks is to have a magnet, and that magnet is media/communication/journalism studies. The problem is quite large, as the late Michael Crichton pointed out to a Commonwealth Club audience in October 2003: "The greatest challenge facing mankind is the challenge of distinguishing reality from fantasy, truth from propaganda. Perceiving the truth has always been a challenge to mankind, but in the information age (or as I think of it, the disinformation age) it takes on a special urgency and importance." Media studies, Marshall McLuhan once said, provide civil defense against media fallout.

---

[29] David Plotz, "We Are in a Golden Age for Journalism," *National Post*, May 27, 2014, http://news.nationalpost.com/full-comment/david-plotz-we-are-in-a-golden-age-for-journalism.
[30] Richard Saul Wurman, *Information Anxiety* (New York: Doubleday, 1989), 6.

2

SOCIAL MEDIA IN THE AGE OF GLOBAL INFORMATION WARFARE

In case you missed it, your privacy is gone. Under conditions of omnipresent, always-on media, the nature of the system is to convert the medium of full disclosure into users of full disclosure. Already you are primed for this with reality TV shows, *American Idol* and *Britain's Got Talent*, and the perpetual demographic and psychographic marketing machines known as Facebook, Twitter, Instagram, etc. Any social media outlet that is free is just like any television channel that is free: the content is you; and your behaviors, habits, click-through links, and spending patterns are precisely the datasets that are being tracked and sold through giant corporations like Acxiom, Rapleaf, Intelius, Pipl, and the credit score agencies Equifax, TransUnion, and Experian.[1] Chances are good these companies already know more about you than your mother does.

As the satirical newspaper *The Onion* put it, Facebook is a "massive online surveillance program run by the CIA" and rewarded its director, Mark Zuckerberg, because he has persuaded people to voluntarily reveal a depth and level of personal information that used to take years and years to compile.[2] And make no

---

[1] David Goldman, "These Data Miners Know Everything about You," CNN Money, December 16, 2010, http://money.cnn.com/galleries/2010/technology/1012/gallery.data_miners/index.html.
[2] "CIA's 'Facebook' Program Dramatically Cut Agency's Costs," *The Onion* video, 3:43, accessed August 24, 2017, http://www.theonion.com/video/cias-facebook-program-dramatically-cut-agencys-cost-19753.

mistake; the joke is as funny as it is tragic. The very concept of privacy in the digital age is so anomalous that now the person not on Facebook is considered suspect. Unless she's Amish, what is there to hide? For most digital kids, the unphotographed plate of food is not worth eating, the unshared moment is not worth having, and the untweeted life is not worth living.

But this also is a good moment to observe how changes in media form are correlated to the changing nature of warfare itself:

Orality—Tribal War
Literacy—Land War
Printing—Naval War
Electronic—Air War
Digital—Information War

As the progression reveals, each subsequent form of media encapsulates and absorbs each previous form. Just as digital media contains within itself all previous forms of media, so too does information warfare create a coherent coordination of all air, sea, and land conditions in order to be controlled. You can also see the above block-text progression as a chart of how the world went from multiple nation-states to one global superpower. It is only under conditions of information warfare that one nation-state can become the world's only superpower. The two reinforce each other quite naturally: power needs information to stay in power; information needs power to gather more information. The more information, the more power; and the more power, the more information.

Tomorrow you might check in to the TSA (Transportation Safety Administration) with your Facebook or any other number of social media apps. Already you can see that through an aggregation of your Facebook profile, your eBay rating, your credit score, your travel history, and your social media presence, the nation-state would have no real trouble discerning who was and was not a threat to air travel. This is one reason why law enforcement agencies are always retroactively looking at social media feeds for clues as to what was going through the attacker's mind after a terrorist event. In the future, law enforcement will look a lot more like the film *Minority Report*. All of your musical, cinematic, fashion, religious, economic, cultural, lifestyle, and personal "likes" will be fed through a master grid that aggregates and analyzes the likelihood of criminal behavior based on pattern-recognition programs that "predict" future scenarios based on past events. In many ways, those programs are already up and running; they're just currently being used to push you more weirdly specific advertisements in your sidebar.

CAN THE GOOD LIFE BE VIRTUALIZED?

It is a strange fact of the human condition that one organ only—the mouth—should serve two completely separate functions. The ear only hears, the eye only sees, the nose only smells, but the mouth of man is the strangest of strange organs, for it is both a consumer and a producer: it is an input mechanism for food and simultaneously an output mechanism for words. The tongue is that odd, multitasking organ that both tastes your food and flavors your speech.

Since that original, God-given medium of speech, mankind has altered its speech by altering its medium for speech in specific historical instances, which mankind has taken fondly to calling (among other things) "technological progress." And since the time of Christ, we know that what goes into the mouth of man is not what makes him evil, but what comes out of his mouth that originates not from the stomach, but from the heart. So if the kingdom of God is not food and drink, and out of the abundance of the heart the mouth speaks, then Christian liberal-arts students should be wary, lest they become what they behold, or as Mom put it, "You are what you eat." So consuming a supersaturated media diet while simultaneously attempting to articulate the gospel to this present age may make us sound to the host culture like we are talking with our mouths full. And if time is the currency of love, then our 8–12 daily hours of electronic mass media consumption may be the best indicator of the peculiar shape of our love in this age, and raises essential questions about how our choices feed in us the truest self—the image of the living Word—or simply fatten and reinforce the falseness that obscures the shape of true incarnation.

The critical danger for this rising generation that some call "digital natives" is the risk of several identifiable psychological disorders as a result of spending more time in the virtual world than in the real world. In the face of these real dangers, crafting an embodied response—choosing to offer the presence of incarnational communication to a world suffering from its absence—becomes the most serious and vital work young Christians can engage in. Being in but not of the virtual world is, at the most basic level, the difference between life and death. There are at least six observable vices of the virtual life that we should vigilantly watch for in ourselves, our friends, and our loved ones.

DISEMBODIMENT

The primary noticeable media effect of our age, and perhaps the key to understanding and/or the cause of all the other effects is *disembodiment*. On the phone, on the web, on TV, you are simultaneously everywhere and nowhere. This creates a mind-body separation that both mimics death and parodies angels, eliminates the possibility of natural law, and allows you to become pure "information," simply wearing the corporate body as your own. Indeed, the student's struggle with pornography and/or masturbation and the student's struggle with body image and/or cutting may simply be an attempt to get back "in touch" with his or her disembodied self as a means of verifying or proving one's physical existence. "I achieve self-stimulated orgasm, therefore I am" and "I feel self-stimulated pain, therefore I am" may become the new Cartesian existential veracities.

The disembodiment of digital media also results in an isola-tion and absence from the group. Sherry Turkle's book *Alone Together* documents this quite well. But if you've ever pondered why so-called "social media" preemptively requires you to engage in "antisocial behavior" by being alone at your computer, then you're already conscious of the paradox. And for the Christian whose identity consists in imitating the incarnated Christ, this represents a grave danger. Our entire religion rests on the fantastical claim of the virtual made real, the idea of an invisible God actually and literally embodying himself in the physical presence of one his-torically real human being, Jesus Christ. If true, then Christ really is the antibody to the virus of mass disincarnation. This is what both the incarnation and Communion are all about, and why the Christian faith may be more crucial for sanity in the digital world than ever before.

DESENSITIZATION

Desensitization wasn't so much a problem for the oral age (then–3500 BC), writing age (3500 BC–AD 1439), or print age (1439–1839). But since then, it's become a growing concern. The electronic age (1839–2007) is the one your professors were born into. You were born into the digital age (2007–present), and that is sometimes why you seem to speak a different language than we professors do. I was born, for instance, just four years after the term "information over-load" was coined (1964), which was a communication technology version of the 1950s term "sensory overload." You were born, by contrast, within a few years of the first use of the phrase "apoca-lypse fatigue" (1992). So while your professors were born into the struggle of managing all this newly available information, you were born into the struggle of how to deal with the psychological effects of all this information. And looking to your professors for help in solving the second problem, while they're still working on the first one, has admittedly been disappointing. We feel it too. Desensitization is a risk for everyone in the digital environment.

"Apocalypse fatigue" is kin to the term "empathy fatigue," which first originated as a description for grief counselors who were trying to help too many students deal with losses associated with school shootings. These days, empathy fatigue is no longer associated with the emotional shutdown that accompanies an acute crisis. It is simply the birthright of a generation whose human organism lacks the innate apparatus to filter and absorb the omnipresent psychic stimulation of the digital age. It is what happens when a mortal is required to shoulder digitally delivered "omniscience." We were created to handle the stories and sorrows of the tribe we were born into. Under digital conditions, we're required to somehow shoulder the weight of a global knowledge—it is a psychic overstimulation that exhausts our ability to remain fully present.

As Marshall McLuhan put it, if the price of liberty is eternal vigilance, then the price of vigilance is indifference. So if the pop singer Roger Waters had become "comfortably numb" by 1979, then it's little wonder that the Kaiser Chiefs in 2008 were singing, "It's cool to know nothin'." With so much to care about, one of the primary frustrations for students is a world of adults telling them to care about this or that or the other. One of the chief complaints of Christian-college students regarding chapel is the sense of helpless frustration they feel after hearing a year's worth of chapel talks. It's not that they don't care or want to care about any given speaker's concerns; it's that the collective effect of all those concerns leaves them with a feeling of emotional paralysis that borders on despair. At Christian colleges, students come to resent what they call "chapeltisements," not because they don't care about the issues, but because they can't care—it is impossible for one person to possibly care about every single issue and remain sane.

Scripture tells us that with more knowledge comes more sorrow (Eccles. 1:18), and digital media is nothing if not a knowledge multiplier. How to care at all when there's too much to care about is most likely going to be one of the great struggles of your entire life.

NARCISSISM

Another media effect, *narcissism*, is a term often bandied about as simply being a heightened version of vanity or egotism, but it is in fact something more significant, bordering on solipsism. We do live in a world of choices that revolve around our egos, from YouTube to MySpace to iPods and "my.school.edu" or "my.bank.com" or "my.healthcare.com." But the bigger evidence of narcissism is the way in which the online self is a created second self, and the way that narcissism is the careful crafting of a grandiose "false self" to cover over or protect the "true self" from wounding. If you're just a regular kid during the week, but a god on Facebook or World of Warcraft, then your second self may be bigger than your first, and your second self may indeed meet the qualifications of being a false self to protect your true self from perceived threats or weaknesses. If you've taken more than one photograph of yourself for your Facebook profile to capture just the right you in just the right light from just the right angle, then you've already experienced the phenomenon.

If we are to take no thought for tomorrow, for what we'll eat or wear or do, then how do we reconcile this with an obsession with how we look in our second life? Christians are to be known by their charitable altruism in sacrificing self for the benefit of other selves. If we are known by our avatars, how will we be known by our love?

While narcissism may appear to be an aggrandizing of the self, it is, ironically, evidence of a profound loss of identity. In the oral age, there was a seamlessness between individuals' essential selves and the words they spoke. In the digital world, when our words are spoken, written, typed, texted, and tweeted, they may refer to any number of our multiple selves, causing ourselves and others to wonder which of us is the true self. Since the invention of the first mass medium in 1455 (the book), mankind has been threatened with losing a singular identity in the presence of mediated alternatives. "Schizophrenia may be a necessary consequence of literacy," Marshall McLuhan argued back in 1961. Indeed, the term *doppelganger* goes back to the eighteenth century. Since then, the options for bifurcating the self under digital conditions have multiplied to the point where we now look at multiple-personality disorder not as a disease but as a form of entertainment, from Lady Gaga's accelerated costume changes in her videos to the TV show *The United States of Tara*, about a mother with dissociative identity disorder. In the third season, there are two new personalities introduced to complement the existing four personalities of the main character.

Remember, Christ is the singular source of identity and salvation; it is Satan who is legion. If we are to have our identity in one and only one source, Christ, then these new media forms present us with the danger of becoming disordered Christians with multiple personalities.

PASSIVITY

Probably the most easily diagnosed media effect, and the one that the average student feels intuitively, is *passivity*. It is often described with the line, "I'm not feeling it."

The average American spends 8–12 hours in media consumption—that represents at least half of all waking hours spent in passively consuming culture rather than actively producing it. Just the American TV habit of 35 hours per week is almost equivalent to a second full-time job. Even the alleged blessing of the two-way new media (such as blogging, Facebook, Twitter, and others) primarily consists of regurgitating other people's content rather than any real artistic or intellectual originality.

Selective exposure to our chosen media streams can give us the perception of being permanently in the present tense and deprive us of the sense of time passing. This can create a feeling that our options are perpetually open, when in fact time and fortune are passing us by the minute. Cultural engagement, civic participation, voter turnout, and other markers all show signs of decreasing instead of increasing. On a long enough time line, passivity can lead to a goallessness that can manifest as either the hyperactivity of going nowhere that Mark Edmundson calls "possibility junkies," or the regression found in thirty-five-year-olds still living at home with Mom's cooking and laundry service. If we are to be salt and light and yeast in the world, Christians are called to get out there and agitate things, to afflict the comfortable and comfort the afflicted, and to be in it but not of it. One way to do this is to get off the couch, get off the web, get off the phone, and go do something.

IGNORANCE

A fifth problem is the fact that all of these knowledge products are demonstrably making us dumber, stupider, and more idiotic than ever before. This growing *ignorance* is documented in several recent books, from Mark Bauerlein's *The Dumbest Generation* to *Idiot America* by Charles P. Pierce to *Just How Stupid Are We?* by Rick Shenkman. Suffice it to say, the evidence is all around that we are not getting any smarter by virtue of all this knowledge technology. Almost all measures of intelligence, from fluid to crystallized intelligence, long- and short-term memory, reading and writing skills, etc., are all dependent on the functioning of mind, memory, and language. When the contents of mind, memory, and language can be externalized in a medium like "the cloud," and portable media devices give us the illusion of portable omniscience, we are really shifting the contents of our brains from an internal to an external hard drive, and our brains are getting softer in the process. This also helps explain why students nationwide resent assessments that test their hard command of facts and, more than ever, don't understand why plagiarism is an issue.

We become *idiots* in the root sense of the word—highly

individualized people who have a very private knowledge set that may not be shared or valued by anyone else in the culture. It's not that the village idiot can't have a meaningful conversation; it's that his conversation is only meaningful to himself. Taken together, the result of digitally induced idiocy is a culture that values the individual over the group, when the history of civilized cultures tells a fairly consistent story of balance between the good of the group (the "greater good") and the good of the individual. If the root meaning of *communication* is community, then idiocy and community are clearly at odds.

INSTANT GRATIFICATION

In a digitally accelerated, point-and-click media world, you're going to want things faster, sooner, now. *Instant gratification* is the blessing of most digital technology; it is also its collective curse. If you've ever complained about your school's Internet connection speed, or if you bought the iPad 2 just to get the 3-second faster start-up time over the first iPad, then you know the feeling. The problem is that literacy, personality, many moral traits, and civilization itself are all built upon the assumptions of deferred gratification.

Deferred gratification is the patient willingness to build in incremental slow steps toward an eventual outcome. With the rise of instant-gratification media forms, we see the loss of the old, deferred-gratification arts, including but not limited to letter writing, calligraphy, representational realism in art, model building, and book reading. But pyramids and cathedrals are all built on the foundation of deferred gratification, along with many other products of cultural value, from Yo-Yo Ma's cello playing to single-malt Scotch. Indeed, heaven itself and the Christian faith can be seen as one long exercise in deferred gratification, "a long obedience in the same direction," to use Eugene Peterson's phrase.[3] The best

---

[3] Eugene Peterson, *A Long Obedience in the Same Direction: Discipleship in an Instant Society* (Downers Grove, IL: InterVarsity Press, 2000).

antidote to the hazards of instant gratification is to cultivate a skill or a hobby that you can't get good at within one year. Then do it again, several times throughout your life.

Taken collectively, these six vices are really unintended consequences of otherwise marvelous technologies. But when you add them all up, they really can produce an absurd species inhabiting an absurd culture, intent on what Neil Postman described as "amusing ourselves to death."[4] Digitally deprived of our autonomy, maturity, and identity, we can become an infantilized culture motivated by the newest media stimulus that produces a physiologically forced response. It sounds pretty bleak, of course. But McLuhan said that "there is absolutely no inevitability as long as there is a willingness to contemplate what is happening,"[5] and Jacques Ellul said that the purpose of real religion was to call the sleeper to awake.[6] If Christians wake from the somnambulistic trance that modern mass media has put us into, then perhaps we can be of use to a mass culture seemingly intent on sleepwalking itself off the cliff. If it was for freedom that Christ set us free, then it is crucial to consider that the medium of Christ's message was embodied communication, and that this may indeed be the only salvation from an otherwise technologically determined enslavement.

It is important to realize that we do not sin when we create or participate in mass media or technological progress. But, we do need to remember that Jesus is the Word. In a sense, the foundational work that underlies everything else we do is to answer T. S. Eliot's questions: "Where will the word resound?" and "Where is the wisdom we have lost in knowledge?"[7] In the digital age, we have deepened the problem: Where is the knowledge we have lost in data? In a certain sense, since the exile from Eden, we have fixed

---

[4] Neil Postman, *Amusing Ourselves to Death: Public Discourse in the Age of Show Business* (New York: Penguin, 1985).

[5] Marshall McLuhan, *The Medium Is the Massage* (Bantam Books, 1967).

[6] Jacques Ellul, *The Technological Society* (New York: Vintage Books, 1964), xxxiii.

[7] T. S. Eliot, "Choruses from 'The Rock'," 1934.

what wasn't broken, and it has broken us in the process. If Jesus had food that we didn't know about, and it was to do the will of his Father, then perhaps the healthiest media diet is really that simple: to walk, talk, and act in our embodied selves as Christ did among the poor, the sick, and the outcast. We need to quiet ourselves long enough to hear the whisper that will tell us what food will nourish us deeply, and what food will only stuff our mouths and make it impossible to really speak.

3

CHRISTIAN IDENTITY AS THE ANTIDOTE TO DIGITAL IDENTITY

A CHRISTIAN ECOLOGY OF THE EAR-EYE RELATIONSHIP

This concept of the arts as prophetic, contrasts with the popular idea of them as mere self-expression.

Marshall McLuhan[1]

This life's dim windows of the soul
Distorts the heavens from pole to pole
And leads you to believe a lie
When you see with, not through, the eye.

William Blake[2]

Yet the aim of art is to represent not the outward appearance of things, but their inward significance; for this, and not the external mannerism and detail, is their reality.

Will Durant[3]

The Son is the image of the invisible God . . .

Colossians 1:15 (NIV)

---

[1] Marshall McLuhan, *Understanding Media: The Extensions of Man* (New York: McGraw-Hill, 1964), x.
[2] William Blake, "The Everlasting Gospel" in *The Complete Poetry and Prose of William Blake,* ed. David Erdman (Oakland: University of California Press, 2008), 520.
[3] Will Durant, *The Story of Philosophy: The Lives and Opinions of the Great Philosophers of the Western World* (1929; repr., New York: Simon and Schuster, 2005), 59.

If agriculture is the root of all metaphor, then the kingdom of God is like an earthy story.[4] It is a parable that you have not heard yet, but that, upon hearing, feels very familiar because it makes use of all the signs and signifiers of your current life while asking you to consider your situation in the here and now and to make a choice regarding where you will be at the outcome of the story.

When Jesus tells his parables in Matthew 13, they are all imaginative stories about what the kingdom of God is like, yet they all address the question of lived reality in the current cultural context of the story's audience and never speak of an ideal state of heaven in the sweet by and by. The parables of the kingdom in Matthew 13 are all stories about the heavenly realm, yet they all employ strictly earthbound metaphors, analogies, and symbols. As such, they make no explicit demands on their audience, and yet they simultaneously pose an implicit question to each listener: Who are you in this story? For those with ears to hear, these stories demand an answer only to the questions the hearer asks herself, which requires the participation of the listener in real time. In this way, all of these parables convert the audience members into characters in the story, whose choices and attitudes have a present, real, and significant role to play in determining whether the story and its outcome is ultimately a comedy or a tragedy.

Here is Jesus's list of qualifications necessary to understand, believe, and participate in the kingdom that his parables speak of:

He who has ears to hear, let him hear. (Matt. 11:15)

No PhD, no advanced study, no sophistication—just a set of ears. In fact, in the same chapter, Jesus goes on to say,

. . . I praise you, Father, Lord of heaven and earth, because you have hidden these things from the wise and learned, and revealed

---

[4] Much of the material in this chapter comes from my lecture "What Are Communication Scholars Telling Us about the Source and Role of the Imagination?" (lecture, Billy Graham Center and Marion E. Wade Center Evangelism Roundtable, Wheaton, IL, April 23–26, 2008).

them to little children. Yes, Father, for this is what you were pleased to do. (Matt. 11:25–26 NIV)

Or, as Marshall McLuhan put it in 1970,

> . . . it is visible to babes, but not to sophisticates. The sophisticated, the conceptualizers, the Scribes and the Pharisees—these had too many theories to be able to perceive anything. Concepts are wonderful buffers for preventing people from confronting any form of percept.[5]

If contemporary Christians wish to transmit a meaningful gospel to a world awash in meaningless media, then they have a dual dilemma to confront before they can hope to proceed successfully. The first is that they must understand how the evolution of the medium of transmission affects the meaning and reception of the message of the gospel. The second is that they must understand whether technological change necessitates a methodological change in storytelling, or whether there is a timeless principle in Scripture upon which to make effective media for Christ and his kingdom, regardless of the age in which one lives. Christians must look through their media rather than at it, and they must create media that encourages the receiver to look through rather than at, if they wish it to be effective.

Another way of posing the problem is revealed in the layers of God's presence with man. From an audible presence in the garden to a visible, physical form in Christ to a testimony of those appearances in Scripture, we must pay significant attention to the subtle shifts in perspective that happen depending on which layer we are looking at. Christ gave up his body and blood to be new food and drink for us, yet too many in our world find the sacrament incomprehensible to the point of meaningless because they see it as a symbol (grape juice and cracker) of a symbol (bread and wine) of

---

[5] Marshall McLuhan, Eric McLuhan, and Jacek Szklarek, eds., *The Medium and the Light: Reflections on Religion* (Toronto: Stoddart, 1999), 83.

a symbol (body and blood). In this way, the gospel of Christianity can, to the outsider, often look indistinguishable from the fakery of the technological world, the world—described by Chuck Palahniuk as one in which everything is "a copy of a copy of a copy,"[6] a world in which everything is so far removed from its original source as to be entirely detached to the point of being unrecognizable. This is the same problem articulated by the French theorist Jean Baudrillard in his four stages of the image: the devolution from representation to pure simulacrum[7] is a problem that is uniquely ours in the digital age.

To be sure, contemporary Christians have gone a long way in adding to, supplementing, and sophisticating the message since Christ's time in order to be as relevant, authentic, and effective as possible to today's jaded, bored, distracted, and ADDled potential parishioners. Enter any electronically amplified and Jumbotroned megachurch and you will see what Guy Debord called "the spectacle"[8] on full display. Put another way, it is a gazillion-channel universe.

Adjacent to and deeply enmeshed in this universe of media saturation and fragmentation lies the planet's most popular religion, a parallel world of 1.5 billion self-identifying Christians, 800 million of whom are Protestants, which are divided into (at last count in 2001) over 33,000 denominations in 238 countries with between 270 and 300 new denominations added each year.[9] This means that currently there are over 37,500 denominations communicating the gospel through their chosen media to Christians worldwide.

But if the word *communicate* shares the same root with the words *communion* and *community*—"to make many one"—then perhaps something is getting lost in translation. For the result of all

---

[6] Chuck Palahniuk, *Fight Club* (New York: Henry Holt, 1996), 96.
[7] Jean Baudrillard, *Simulacra and Simulation* (Ann Arbor, MI: University of Michigan Press, 1995), 6.
[8] Guy Debord, *The Society of the Spectacle* (New York: Zone, 1995).
[9] David Barrett, George Kurian, and Todd Johnson, *World Christian Encyclopedia: A Comparative Survey of Churches and Religions in the Modern World* (Oxford: Oxford University Press, 2001).

this effort at mediated relevance, authenticity, and effectiveness has not been, historically speaking, a growing unification of the splintered church, but paradoxically, an acceleration of the splintering. In order to understand and counter this trend, Christians should face squarely the task of questioning the relationship between the medium of communication and the message of the gospel, between the increase in media channels and the simultaneous and seemingly parallel increase in Protestant audiences, and between these elements and their relationship to imaginative storytelling and, therefore, effective Christian witness.

Christians should be in the creative arts. We are made in God's image. We should remake the world in that image. That much, many Christians agree on. Marshall McLuhan, a devout Christian and a founding father of the field of media ecology, said of himself that he was never a scholar or academic but only an artist. "The serious artist," McLuhan claimed, "is the only person able to encounter technology with impunity, just because he is an expert aware of the changes in sense perception."[10] What is less agreed on is how remaking the world in "that image" should be done, as there is both a great history and tradition of remaking the world in God's image, and a great history and tradition in remaking the world in man's image. Worse still, there is a great history and tradition of men attempting to remake the world in God's image, but limited to the use of merely human means, unwittingly making the form in man's image while the content is supposedly made in God's image, resulting in a new cultural context that is often centered around man's creation and control of God-centered media.

If we are to be artists, to be image-makers cognizant of our unique role as image-bearers, then it is of great significance that we seriously consider the question asked of the artist: What is your medium? McLuhan claimed the principle that "we become what

---

[10] Marshall McLuhan, *Understanding Media: The Extensions of Man* (New York: McGraw-Hill, 1964), 33.

we behold, we shape our tools and thereafter our tools shape us."[11] This was a biblical principle McLuhan took from the 115th Psalm:[12]

> Their idols are silver and gold, the work of men's hands.
> They have mouths, but they speak not: eyes have they, but they
> see not:
> They have ears, but they hear not: noses have they, but they
> smell not:
> They have hands, but they handle not; feet have they, but they
> walk not: neither speak they through their throat.
> They that make them shall be like unto them; so is every one
> that trusteth in them. (Ps. 115:4–8 KJV)

McLuhan's commentary on this verse is:

> The concept of "idol" for the Hebrew Psalmist is much like that
> of Narcissus for the Greek mythmaker. And the Psalmist insists
> that the beholding of idols, or the use of technology, conforms
> men to them.[13]

Do different material media means affect different spiritual ends? This question is worthy of a careful investigation from both a biblical perspective and from the perspective of our current cultural context in history, precisely because there is too much evidence to allow us any longer to sustain the old naïveté. The answer that is naïve, I believe, is the one that says, "Any medium is fine, so long as it is done to the glory of God." This strikes me as the road of good intentions, a road whose destination we are all familiar with. It is the world all around us. It is the world in which the classical arts, for example, are increasingly overwhelmed by and drowned out of the culture by economically driven electronic media, for

---

[11] Ibid., 54–55.

[12] Ironically, McLuhan has this misquoted in his text as Psalm 113, when it is in fact Psalm 115:4–8. Given McLuhan's devout Catholicism, one supposes this mistake was the function of an *almost* perfect biblical memory, combined with the fact that his wife, who did all of his editing, would most likely never have suspected it to be an error. (But this is purely my own speculation.)

[13] McLuhan, *Understanding Media*, 45.

whom profit and marketability are the highest arbiters of beauty, truth, and goodness. For Marshall McLuhan, "The conventional response to all media, namely that it is how they are used that counts, is the numb stance of the technological idiot."[14] Jacques Ellul warns that, for Christians, the stakes are even higher: "A statement by the church that it is placing the media at the service of Christ, is not a logical or ethical explanation, but a pious formula without content."[15]

Since all things are permissible (cf. 1 Cor. 10:23), contemporary Christians have had a tendency to assume that all new media forms are inherently beneficial if used for the promotion of the gospel. Or, they think that somehow, by being put to use for the gospel, the new media forms will change their inherent structure and bias in acquiescence to the power of the gospel. It is a case of Christian anthropomorphism with tragic results. You can baptize a prostitute and she may leave her prostitution as a result—but this is because, inherent in her humanity, she has the possibility of agency, the reality of freedom to choose. But if you baptize a technology and say, "Henceforward you shall be used only for the good of the gospel," there is literally nothing about it that can possibly change as a result of the new acceptance—because inherent in its structure is exactly zero possibility of agency, of conforming to good intentions. It is like trying to reform a gun: it will not convert from being a tool of death to a tool of healing as a result of an imposed salvation. It will not because it cannot: it will remain evermore a gun, designed for one thing only. The earnestness, sincerity, and deep emotion we may attach to its conversion won't matter one bit. And this belief—that new media, once baptized by sincere Christians, are but new and improved delivery mechanisms for the timeless truth of Scripture—is not even warranted by Scripture.

Regarding the use of modern communication techniques for

---

[14] Ibid., 32.
[15] Jacques Ellul, *Propaganda: The Formation of Men's Attitudes* (New York: Vintage, 1965), 231.

the church, Jacques Ellul said, "What is in the service of Jesus Christ receives its character and effectiveness from Jesus Christ."[16] And it is the principle of incarnational presence that, above all things, distinguishes the "character and effectiveness" of Christ, if for no other reason than that incarnational presence was the prerequisite for all his other modes of effective action. This is the clear and consistent story of Scripture from John 1:1 to John 3:16, from the Old Testament's prophecies of Christ's coming to the New Testament's prophecy of his second coming. God's love was so strong that he came out of spiritual form and took on a material, embodied form and dwelt among us. His real presence was incarnated—enrobed in flesh—and he resided with us in time and space and matter (cf. John 1:14). If we are to be imitators of Christ (cf. Eph. 5:1–2), then this principle of incarnational presence is one that should precede and predicate any discussion of Christian use of new media. This means that our primary task is to be the embodied gospel to any individual we encounter, and our creation of media can only be, by definition, a secondary and lesser effort, with secondary and lesser effects. It is the ground and being of our life, more than the figure of our creative output, that will have primacy in changing hearts. As the poet Annie Johnson Flint put it,

> We are the only Bible the careless world will read;
> We are the sinner's gospel, we are the scoffer's creed;
> We are the Lord's last message, given in deed and word;
> What if the type is crooked? What if the print is blurred?[17]

From an artistic perspective, Christ was a master at looking through a situation before deciding what to give his audience to look at. If looking at something necessarily implies a surface-level understanding—something arrested in time and no longer

---

[16] Ibid.

[17] Annie Johnson Flint, "The World's Bible," in Edward MacHugh, *Edward MacHugh's Treasury of Gospel Hymns and Poems* (Chicago: The Rodeheaver, Hall-Mack Company, 1938), 109.

flexible—then looking through something implies a penetration into what Durant (who was writing of Aristotle) called the "inward significance" of things, or what Christians understand as the "eternally present truth." This is the difference between the letter of the law that kills, and the spirit of the law that gives life (cf. 2 Cor. 3:6).

Over and over again, we see Jesus resisting forms of communication that calcify meaning. We see this in almost every encounter he has, whether with the woman at the well, the rich man, the soldier, the disciples, the Pharisees, or Pontius Pilate. Perhaps the closest Christ came to an "artist's statement" is the moment he chose to remain silent in answer to Pilate's question, "What is truth?" (John 18:38). It is at that moment, in the unique context of being the King of kings asked to give an answer for himself to a king of men (in a context that is perceived by Pilate as just the opposite—as a king asking a peasant for a respectful and fearful answer), that Christ chose silence, and in so doing revealed the medium (himself, the Logos or Word) and not the message (his words or statements) as the question's answer. Essentially, the answer that Jesus gave to Pilate is that presence, his presence, is the only complete answer to the question, and that silence in the face of temporal authority is the only way to articulate the embodied Word with heavenly authority. It is clear from Pilate's reaction to Christ's continued silence later on (John 19:9), that no words of Christ could have shocked Pilate more. As Matthew 27:14 tells it, "But Jesus made no reply, not even to a single charge—to the great amazement of the governor" (NIV).

Christ's refusal to let living words be calcified may offer a clue for our use and understanding of media. Perhaps the deadening effect of the letter of the law and the enlivening effect of the spirit of the law are directly related to media forms: written words are themselves the inflexible, dry, desiccated remnants of the once-embodied speech they represent. Living words—words revitalized by a living speaker, in context—can offer hope, joy, and solace from an otherwise foregone conclusion. This is Christ's liberation to the woman caught in adultery in John 8:1–11. The written law (cf. Deut. 22:22–24) had predicted the outcome of death by stoning. Christ refused this legalistic fatality by changing the medium of the law from the written word to the living embodiment of sinlessness.

The purpose of law is to serve as a neutral, objective, and detached form upon which the content of moral and social justice is derived, but Christ saw through the Pharisees' attempt to use the law as a tool for a very subjective purpose—the gloating desire to enjoy a public stoning. They left humbled and, one presumes, awed by Christ's authority. As he himself is the living embodiment of the law, it is his authority that allows him to play the role of judge, jury, and not—contra the written law—executioner. But Christ did not leave the woman's sin untouched. Rather, he said, "Go, and sin no more" (John 8:11 KJV).

In the larger context of Christ's life, this living-word principle may itself offer a clue as to why Christ—who likely would have studied the law as a young man—would neither write down nor encourage his followers to write down anything he said. Neither does the Great Commission include literacy per se as one of its necessary ingredients. Since that moment, however, as McLuhan puts it, "the missionaries took alphabetic literacy wherever they went along with the gospel, even though the two have nothing to do with each other."[18]

In other words, textual transmission of the gospel is secondary to embodiment of Christ. And while contemporary Christians may not be able to achieve this embodiment without first having the help of the mediated text, we must never forget that the original Christians were not basing their lives on written texts, but on new revelations experienced during their real lives, delivered to them through a living medium. Christ's incarnational presence,

---

[18]Marshall McLuhan, *The Video McLuhan, Tape 2: 1965–1970* (Toronto: McLuhan Productions, 1996), VHS.

in effect, liberated his followers' enslavement to the dead medium and legalism of the Old Testament by offering a new and living interpretation. It was shocking precisely because it was so novel, so unscripted, so unsettling to the tradition that had been handed down by centuries of writing and the habits engendered thereby. It shocks us still, but understood in context, we see more clearly why they felt they had to kill him—he was upsetting the tradition, predictability, and control that writing had created.

And yet Scripture was written down, and our role as Christians is to rehydrate the dry, desiccated husks of Scripture's written words in order to give them embodiment in the life of the world. But our relationship to these words is not as simple as understanding them as dehydrated speech that must be converted to living sounds. For Scripture takes the form of writing, and in these words we find the prohibition on images: the words tell us not to use images. But another level of complexity remains, and it is this: these words are themselves images.

To be specific, in the history of the phonetic alphabet (the sole basis of the oral word made visible in writing and later in print) lies the curious fact that all alphabets began as pictographic symbol systems. The form of letters on a page were originally representative images, but are now so historically abstracted from us as to be invisible: the "A" does not appear to us as a Hebrew Aleph, or *ox*; the "B" does not look like a Bet, or *house* to us; and these visual cues can no longer be triggered by the ancient pictogram from whence each letter derived.[19] When we read, we do not look at the letters with any discernible recognition of meaning. Indeed, phonetic literacy itself requires that we peer through these shapes to the mental construction of their sounds, and from these sounds to the mental comprehension of their meaning.

This distinction between pictographic and phonetic alphabets

---

[19] Leonard Shlain, *The Alphabet Versus the Goddess: The Conflict between Word and Image* (New York: Viking Press, 1998), 64–71. See also Robert Logan, *The Alphabet Effect: The Impact of the Phonetic Alphabet on the Development of Western Civilization* (New York: St. Martin's, 1987).

lies at the heart of what communication scholars call the difference between an *analogical* and a *digital* symbol.[20] Analogical symbols are those that bear a visual analogy with what they represent; digital symbols are those that bear no visual resemblance to what they represent. Scripture, then, is a compilation of images that we think of as words, and yet these very image-words prohibit us from making images (cf. Ex. 20:4; Deut. 5:8). It is a little like fighting fire with charcoal.

The paradox is this: while analogical visual symbols (images) have the tendency in their effects to arrest our vision at the surface of the symbols (rather than allowing us to peer through them), it is nevertheless the case that digital symbols (words) are but analogical symbols abstracted through time. Thus it is crucial to recognize that where we stand in relation to the symbols in time will signify for us how abstractly or literally we are able to read them, and this will tend to determine whether we look at or through them, which in turn tends to determine whether we are using them as icons or idols. In literal fact, we see that the Hebrews gave primacy of place to the ox (aleph), which was the very image of their false god when they impatiently rebelled while waiting for Moses to come down from the mountain (Ex. 32:1–20). This golden calf, when seen through (i.e., seen for what it was, as a false god), still retained a secondary primacy in their symbol system when it became the first letter of their alphabet. In other words, the idolatrous quality of the ox's image was not inherent in the image itself, but inherent in the Hebrews' relationship to it in time.

The new phonetic alphabet, over time, absorbs, encloses, and becomes the container of the old medium and thereby desacralizes the old god. So it is significant that Moses grinds the golden calf to powder, mixes it with water, and forces the Hebrews to drink it (Ex. 32:20). By the end of Scripture, the alphabet itself becomes con-

---

[20] Paul Watzlawick, Janet Beavin, and Don Jackson, *Pragmatics of Human Communication: A Study of Interactional Patterns, Pathologies, and Paradoxes* (New York: W. W. Norton, 1967), 41–48.

tained in the new medium of Christ's authority when the Lord says, "I am the Alpha and the Omega, the first and the last, the beginning and the end" (Rev. 22:13). So the pattern that is revealed is one in which the image (ox) is supplanted by the word (alphabet), and the word (alphabet) is supplanted by the Word (Christ, the logos). In each case a narrative is supplanted by a metanarrative, and in each case the new form contains a trace or remnant of the old form.

When the Lord says, "I am the Alpha and the Omega," he is using the Greek alphabetic letters to indicate "the first and the last." In Hebrew, the equivalent first and last letters would have created the saying, "I am the Aleph and the Taw, the ox and the signature mark." The Hebrew phonetic alphabet, in its progression, is itself a rudimentary history of media evolution, from perceptual god (aleph = ox = golden calf) to primitive literacy (taw = signature mark = beginnings of writing). The Phoenician equivalent of Taw was x, still the symbol used by illiterate people when "signing" their name to a document. Analogically, it may also be worth noting that the Taw is the very image of the cross, in the form of the "capital *T*" cross symbol of a crucifix. In this light, then, the "first and the last" can be seen as a stand-in for the "author and finisher" of our faith, or as two different symbolizations of Christ himself: Christ as Maker of the world (cf. John 1:3), and Christ as sacrificial Savior of the world.

Thus, understanding where we stand in time is crucial for Christians to properly contextualize the symbols we are producing and consuming in relationship to each other and to God. Only by taking this role of contextualization seriously can we imitate Christ seriously in our use of media. For the ancient Israelites, living in a time of single-image production by limited skilled artists, the power of analogical symbols to overwhelm was far greater than it is today, an age characterized by images reproduced and distributed instantly at very low cost. Neil Postman's reflection on the Second Commandment reveals how strong this visual threat could have been perceived in its historical context:

It is a strange injunction to include as part of an ethical system unless its author assumed a connection between forms of human communication and the quality of a culture. We may hazard a guess that a people who are being asked to embrace an abstract, universal deity would be rendered unfit to do so by the habit of drawing pictures or making statues or depicting their ideas in any concrete, iconographic forms.[21]

The dissolution of analogical symbols into visual abstractions is, in a way, a concise summary of art history: What else but this does it mean when we leave a movie or an art gallery and proclaim with a sigh, "Seen it before!"? Clichéd visual images bother us precisely because, through duplication and replication, we are forced to see only their surface, and can only look *at* rather than *through* them. They disallow us to see their inward significance, in part, because of the speed and redundancy with which we encounter them. And it is this very speed and redundancy that are inherent characteristics of almost all electronic media. Electronic media tends to keep our eyes and minds on the surface of things, very fleetingly, before offering us the next thing. As the pundit put it, How can you tell anymore if you have ADD or just a really bad case of the twenty-first century?

Thus, in visual media, perceptual value is also a function of scarcity. A massively repeated visual image, such as a corporate logo, is always under threat of becoming abstracted and therefore invisible to the viewer—one reason why most corporate logos are redesigned every decade or so. Abstract art itself may simply be an effort to immediately deliver us from analogical symbol recognition and place us on the higher plane of going above, beneath, and beyond the merely visual. Cubism, for example, is the attempt to show the visually observed from all angles at once. By presenting a three-dimensional display on the surface of a two-dimensional medium, cubism invites our eyes to see through the surface of two-dimensional art.

---

[21] Neil Postman, *Amusing Ourselves to Death* (New York: Viking Penguin, 1985), 9.

Different scriptural translations offer subtle but significant differences on why the prohibition of images matters. Here is the King James Version of Exodus 20:4–5:

> Thou shalt not make unto thee any graven image, or any likeness of any thing that is in heaven above, or that is in the earth beneath, or that is in the water under the earth. Thou shalt not bow down thyself to them, nor serve them . . .

Here is the same verse in the New International Version:

> You shall not make for yourself an image in the form of anything in heaven above or on the earth beneath or in the waters below. You shall not bow down to them or worship them . . .

Other versions use the term "carved gods," or in the case of the New Life Version (NLV):

> Do not make for yourselves a god to look like anything that is in heaven above or on the earth below or in the waters under the earth.

With each subsequent translation, from KJV to NIV to NLV, the prohibited item shifts from being a "graven image" (KJV) to "an image" (NIV) to "a god" (NLV). The modern argument ignores this interpretive evolution and typically claims, on the basis of the devolved interpretation, that because this is strictly a reference to godlike images, and since Solomon adorns the doors of the Lord's temple—some five hundred years later—"with carvings of cherubim, palm trees, and open flowers,"[22] then clearly God must not be against images *per se*, but against the use of any image that might make its viewer mistake the image with the thing to be

---

[22] First Kings 6:32 and cf. 2 Chronicles 2, both of which, while descriptive of what Solomon did, are predicated by the Lord's explicit and specific instructions in Exodus 25:8–9: "And let them make me a sanctuary, that I may dwell in their midst. Exactly as I show you concerning the pattern of the tabernacle, and of all its furniture, so you shall make it."

adored. This was culturally understood in the context of Abraham's legacy, which tells of his journey west and the break with his father's tradition, in which Abraham resolved to never again worship gods made by human hands. What the modern argument misses is precisely the way in which the devolving form of the image can create its own idolatry.

In the tension between word and image, then, it would seem our capacity for idolatry is not limited to merely analogical symbols. If the iconoclasts destroyed the icons, paintings, and statuary of medieval churches as a way of remedying what they perceived as the threat to the viewer of mistaking the creation for the Creator, then so too can Protestant history be criticized for unintentionally encouraging a tendency to idolatry of the printed word, as though *sola scriptura* meant "only products of the printing press."

After Gutenberg, the printed Bible quickly became literally mistaken for the words of God, as though the visual symbols on the page were themselves inherently sacred things. As McLuhan put it, "In the sixteenth century and after, many God-fearing readers were sure that the 'inner light' emanated from the black ink of the printed page."[23] But as he explained elsewhere, many of these cultural patterns of perception were themselves a result of the dominant technology:

> The study of the Bible in the Middle Ages achieved conflicting patterns of expression, which the economic and social historian is also familiar with. The conflict was between those who said that the sacred text was a complex unified at the literal level, and those who felt that the levels of meaning should be taken one at a time in a specialist spirit. This conflict between an auditory and a visual bias seldom reached a high degree of intensity until after mechanical and typographical technology had conferred on the visual great preponderance. Prior to this ascendancy, the relative equality among the senses of sight, sound, touch, and movement

---

[23] McLuhan, McLuhan, and Szklarek, *The Medium and the Light*, 90.

in interplay in manuscript culture, had fostered the preference for *light through*, whether in language, art or architecture.[24]

For McLuhan, a lived Christianity, with the living Word of Christ at its center, was the only real "thing" that constituted the faith. This is how he put it, in what was surely one of the most explosive explanations of his aphorism, "The medium is the message," that ever was uttered:

> In fact, it is only at the level of a lived Christianity that the medium really is the message. It is only at that level that figure and ground meet. And that also applies to the Bible: we often speak of the content of Scripture, all while thinking the content is the message. It is nothing of the sort. The content is everybody who reads the Bible: so, in reading it, some people "hear" it, and others don't. All are users of the Word of God, all are its content, but only a small number of them discern its true message. The words are not the message; the message is the effect on us, and that is conversion. In other words, if you read the Bible, how do you read it? Does it pass into your daily life? Only then do you get the message, that is the effect. Only in that moment do medium and message unite.[25]

The iconoclasts had good reason to eliminate the threat to the viewer posed by the multimedia orgy of medieval Catholic churches: their overabundance of visual (as well as auditory and olfactory) scriptural literacy had the effect of making church an opportunity for sensual entertainment as much as or more than an opportunity for humble, penitential, and serious worship. And a significant part of the "protest" part of "Protestantism" was a criticism of the valuing of the image over the Word, a valuing of the signs and symbols of the faith more than the sum and substance of the faith as written in Scripture. And yet, for all it got right, Protestant history does also include a tendency to mistake the symbol

---

[24] Marshall McLuhan, *The Gutenberg Galaxy* (Toronto: University of Toronto Press, 1962), 112–13.

[25] McLuhan, McLuhan, and Szklarek, *The Medium and the Light*, 103.

for the symbolized in the mental equating of the printed-book medium with the content of the gospel. This particular legacy of the Reformation, and the subsequent splintering of the splinter groups into 37,500 separate denominations,[26] is all the more paradoxical for those modern Protestant churches who maintain the ancient creedal belief in the four marks of the church as "one, holy, catholic, and apostolic church." To the outsider, the one true church may be harder to fathom as historical or spiritual reality when it is composed of so many individual churches. And this fact may hamper our witness enormously, even though individuals within these churches may be embodying the gospel faithfully. The outsider may come to church and only taste the shell, rather than the nut of the gospel, as a result of this perception.

Further complicating this word-image tension is the process of visual perception itself in the book medium. A book is, of course, a printed commodity comprised of pages containing symbols that are visually apprehended. But these symbols are the digital offspring of their analogical forebears: as such, their very form requires that we look through them rather than at them in order to read. But this is how we apprehend these symbols only. They are comprehended by passing through their visual imagery and hearing the word sounds in our ears. If this were not so, then we would not all have to be taught, as children, how to read silently (a skill that bewildered me at first, and that James Burke claims was nearly impossible for medieval scribes, and that even Augustine remarked upon when watching Ambrose read silently, as he described it in *The Confessions*). So while visual sight is the primary sense that accesses the symbols, it is the ear that silently "hears" the symbols, decodes, and transmits their meaning to the brain. We might say that the ear, then, is the ultimate goal of the journey that the visual symbols on the page must make for comprehension to be achieved.

---

[26] Barrett, Kurian, and Johnson, *World Christian Encyclopedia*. Add to their numbers the expected annual growth of 270–300.

Just as all written systems evolved from analogical visual symbol systems to abstract alphabets (such as hieroglyphics to Hebrew, in the Israelites' case), so too do all visual images have their true source in the spoken word. The trick, of course, is to remind ourselves that the written word is itself just a visual image, and that unless its dried and desiccated husk is watered and revivified— unless it is spoken, heard, trusted, and obeyed in real time as a living word—then Scripture too can become "just an old book" all too quickly in the living out of our religious faith. This is why church attendance is so prominent and promising for Protestants and can seemingly be so reductionist and formulaic for Catholics: the Protestant needs the service because he needs the sermon to bring the Word to life. The Catholic may be experiencing the Word in a different way throughout the week, and may only go to Mass to receive Holy Communion, resulting in a quick dip in and a just-as-quick exit.

The Protestant's five solas (Scripture alone, faith alone, grace alone, Christ alone, and for the glory of God alone) do not require the Roman Church's "tradition" in order to interpret, which is another way of saying—in media-theory terms—that the oral tradition has nothing to offer that will enlighten the written tradition. In plain terms, it means that Christianity 2.0 obsolesced Christianity 1.0. As Umberto Eco puts it, "Catholic fundamentalism cannot exist—and this is what the Counter Reformation was all about— because for Catholics the interpretation of the Scriptures is mediated by the Church."[27] Thus, for Catholics, all written texts must be mediated by the oral authority of the Roman Catholic Church; for Protestants, the written authority of Scripture is its own authority and is all one needs to unmediate the ecclesiastical hierarchy and authority of oral interpretation.

This primacy of hearing is confirmed by the fact that in common experience, hearing has as its object an immaterial thing,

---

[27] Umberto Eco, *Turning Back the Clock* (London: Vintage Random House, 2008), 281.

whereas sight has as its object a material thing whose existence is empirically tangible. What I see I can touch; what I hear I can only believe. The location of the perceptual organs reveals this: in hearing, the organs are on either side of the head and, by their function, they place the perceiver immediately into the center of perception. In seeing, by contrast, the organs are on the front of the head, facing forward, and the perceiver is always outside of the visual event, as a voyeur peering in.

The tangibility of the visible is confirmed by touch, combined with persistence of visibility after touch, whereas the intangibility of the audible is confirmed by its nonpersistence in audibility once it has been heard. "Did you hear that?" is a question that can only be asked once of a sound (unless it is a repeated sound, like a tapping). Of a sight, we can ask "Did you see that?" repeatedly until the viewer looks at what we see and affirms it (unless it is a disappearing sight, such as a moving jet). As Walter Ong understood it, a primary characteristic of sound is that it goes out of existence as it is heard, whereas sight remains in existence even after it is seen.[28] Thus our relationship to sight and sound in time—our context—is itself dependent on whether we are referring to spoken words or visual images (of which written words are a subset).

This essential difference between the characteristics of sight versus those of sound is significant for another reason, that of value. "You had to be there" is a phrase we say about a live concert; it is not a sentence used in reference to a film or art gallery opening. Visual media (whether still or moving images), because of their inherent persistence in time, often have the dual effect of (a) causing us to merely look at the surface, and (b) causing us to believe that these qualities of persistence and repeat-viewability are proof that they are merely surfaces with no interior depth. In other words, sound media is inherently structured to favor both

---

[28] Walter J. Ong, *Orality and Literacy: The Technologizing of the Word* (New York: Routledge, 1982), 70.

an interiority and a singularity of perception that increases our value of it, whereas visual media is inherently structured to favor both an exteriority and duplicability of perception that decreases our value of it. (Mixed media, such as a film with soundtrack and dialogue, uses techniques to submit both the visual and the aural to the inherent conditions of the visual, which in turn leads to a devaluing of aural media, or what Jacques Ellul called "the humiliation of the word."[29]) There are ways of seeing the interiority of the image, but on contact, images do not immediately suggest to us the possibility of meanings beneath their surfaces. This is seen in the response of the proletariat to abstract art—from indifference to the suggestion that a four-year-old could do that. It is a response that, in effect, says, "This image is not immediately perceptible to my eyes and thus is not worthy of further investigation." Visual art that asks our eyes to do the work of interiority, then, is akin to a literacy requirement for understanding. When this is seen as work, it is often rejected by the casual observer. Kevin Vanhoozer says, "Images may require less work of our imagination."[30] By contrast, images that do require work of our imagination may be preemptively dismissed precisely because they do not strike our eye as immediately perceptible.[31]

Christians are to spread the gospel through word and example, as the *Book of Common Prayer* tells us. Or, as imitators of Christ, who spoke only in word and example. Christ drew in the sand once, but those were words that he drew, not images (John 8:6–8). And Romans 10:17 seems to make the case for a sensory hierarchy that privileges the ear over the eye: "So faith comes from hearing, and hearing through the word of Christ." If we are to know God

---

[29] Jacques Ellul's book of the same name, *The Humiliation of the Word* (Grand Rapids, MI: Eerdmans, 1985), is a magnificent treatise of this particular phenomenon.

[30] Kevin J. Vanhoozer, "The Drama of the Christ: The Gospel as Thing Done and Word Made" (presentation, Gospel and the Imagination Conference, Wheaton College, Wheaton, IL, April 23–26, 2008).

[31] I think of Terrence Malick's film *Tree of Life* (2011) in this regard, something that not until the seventh viewing did I begin to have an "understanding" of.

through Christ, and if Christ is the logos or Word of John 1, then the power of the spoken word, of the heard word, must be much stronger than the seen image.

We know it was in response to spoken words that Lazarus was raised from the dead. We know it was in response to spoken words that the world was created, was called forth into something from nothing. We know from childhood development that hearing is one of the first things babies in utero can do, one reason why modern parents sing and speak and play Mozart for them. We wake up each morning often in response to sound. And we know from the penal system that solitary confinement is one of the cruelest punishments, because it prevents the prisoner from hearing another human being and thus makes him or her literally, all alone. It is also significant that, in America, only 2 percent of the deaf community is Christian.[32] Deaf people can, after all, read and learn to understand through sign language. One question this raises, then, is whether the gospel message is implicitly less powerful, persuasive, or truthful in describing reality when comprehended only visually instead of aurally.

Scripture corroborates the primacy of hearing in its discussion of sight. The story of doubting Thomas in John 20:24–29 is perhaps the most widely referenced example of our modern-day aphorism that "seeing is believing." But what Christ actually says to Thomas in verse 29 suggests a different reading: "Because you have seen me, you have believed; blessed are those who have not seen and yet have believed" (NIV). In this context, it seems that hearing is faith, and that seeing is merely proof. This holds for much of the rest of Scripture. Faith is implicitly defined in relation to hearing in Hebrews 11:1 as "the evidence of things not seen" (KJV), which is to say it is not the evidence of things perceived visually. And this

---

[32] This statement is unverified, but comes from a deaf student at Wheaton College and is also claimed by the Deaf Christian Ministries Foundation of the Midwest.

is true even though God has made himself visible to humanity, at
different periods, from the burning bush to Christ incarnate.

The truth of the visible as the antithesis of faith seems to be in
the response Christ gives to those who ask for a sign in the Gospel
of Matthew:

> When evening comes, you say, "It will be fair weather, for the
> sky is red," and in the morning, "Today it will be stormy, for the
> sky is red and overcast." You know how to interpret the appear-
> ance of the sky, but you cannot interpret the signs of the times.
> A wicked and adulterous generation looks for a sign, but none
> will be given it except the sign of Jonah." (Matt. 16:2–4 NIV)

Later, beginning in verse 8, Christ reminds them of the very visible
sign he gave them with the loaves and the fishes, and he simultaneously reminds them that the point of that sign was not its visible
manifestation, but that it was a pointer to a deeper truth about
eating the yeast of the Pharisees' and Sadducees' teaching:

> Aware of their discussion, Jesus asked, "You of little faith, why
> are you talking among yourselves about having no bread? Do
> you still not understand? Don't you remember the five loaves for
> the five thousand, and how many basketfuls you gathered? Or
> the seven loaves for the four thousand, and how many basket-
> fuls you gathered? How is it you don't understand that I was not
> talking to you about bread? But be on your guard against the
> yeast of the Pharisees and Sadducees." Then they understood
> that he was not telling them to guard against the yeast used in
> bread, but against the teaching of the Pharisees and Sadducees.
> (Matt. 16:8–12 NIV)

In this context, Christ's phrase "you of little faith" almost suggests, "You of little memory and even less comprehension." It is as
if he is saying, "Do you not recall what you saw? And do you not
recall that what you saw was not the point, but that it was pointing
to something beyond itself?" This is confirmed from another angle

in Luke 16:31, when Jesus says, "If they do not listen to Moses and the Prophets, they will not be convinced even if someone rises from the dead" (NIV). Or, in other words, if they do not give heed to what they hear with their ears, nothing demonstrated visibly before their eyes will persuade them.

From a human point of view, of course, it makes sense that his followers kept asking Jesus for a sign—it is simply hard to believe in the reality of the visually observed by just seeing something once, and like a scientific experiment, you want repeatability and predictability to guarantee what you've seen. But living words are spoken words, and inherent in their structure is a singularity of perception in a given moment of time. For a God who is both outside of time and yet is the great "I AM" to his followers, the present tense is the only tense, which may be why Christ's parables in Matthew 13 are so evocative of the listeners' real-time response, and yet have stood the test of time and are now timeless classics that bear repeating two thousand years later (Ex. 3:14).

Scripture also gives us a visual anticipation of the future in 1 Corinthians 13:12. And it is in the distinction between the translation of the New International Version and the King James Version that I think we find our most accurate lens through which to understand God's call on our imagination, our use of media, and especially the dangers and pitfalls of remaining unaware.

The New International Version of the verse reads:

> Now we see only a reflection as in a mirror; then we shall see face to face. Now I know in part; then I shall know fully, even as I am fully known.

The older King James Version of the same verse reads:

> For now we see through a glass, darkly; but then face to face: now I know in part; but then shall I know even as also I am known.

And it is here, in the distinction between a mirror and a glass, between *seeing in* and *seeing through*, that we come to a parable for our times. In our actual image-bearing roles, whether we are present (as image) or speaking (as word), we are faithful witnesses to the gospel so long as we remain true to its teaching. But as soon as we mediate (through our imagination's creative use of the arts), then we must be extremely careful how we use media, lest the form of the mediated symbol begins to work its magic on us unawares.

Protestants have traditionally favored the textually mediated word (in the form of the printed Bible, *sola scriptura*, and the inerrancy doctrine) at the expense of the mediated image (and icons, which Protestants usually view as idols) because of this very distinction. We will "see" fully, of course (i.e., with God's eyes), when we are fully known. Until then, however, both Scripture and experience have made it very apparent that certain media forms favor certain outcomes over others in ways that are remarkably consistent, predictable, and reliable. William Blake put it this way, "I question not my Corporeal or Vegetative Eye any more than I would Question a Window concerning Sight. I look thro' it & not with it."[33]

This does not mean, despite the likelihood of certain outcomes, that Christians should not participate in or produce visual media. It simply means they must be more intentional, aware, and careful of how they do so. There are two scenes, for example, in the 1999 film *American Beauty* that reveal how profoundly delicate, careful, and intentional the visual arts can be in powerfully promoting the gospel to a world gone both deaf and blind by over mediation. They are scenes that specifically relate the visual to the aural, and in doing so, reveal beauty, truth, and goodness in God's world, testify to the fact that God's world contains every aspect of our fallen world, and in that contextual reversal, offer profound insight to Christians attempting to engage the world.

---

[33]William Blake, "A Vision of the Last Judgment," in *Complete Writings*, ed. Geoffrey Keynes (Oxford: Oxford University Press, 1972), 617.

In the movie, the love interest of Jane (the main character's daughter) is the neighbor's strange kid, Ricky Fitts, who videotapes everything he finds worthwhile as he goes through his high school years. As he shows Jane what he calls "the most beautiful thing he's ever filmed," his voiceover describes the scene as we see the moving image of a white plastic bag blown in circles by the wind against the backdrop of a red brick wall. He says,

> It was one of those days when it's a minute away from snowing and there's this electricity in the air, you can almost hear it. And this bag was, like, dancing with me. Like a little kid begging me to play with it. *For fifteen minutes.* And that's the day I knew there was this entire life behind things, and this incredibly benevolent force that wanted me to know there was no reason to be afraid, ever. Video's a poor excuse, I know. *But it helps me remember, and I need to remember . . .* [34]

In the previous scene, the Ricky character has verbally equated "beauty" with "looking God in the face," and does so in a dialogue concerning his filming the face of a homeless woman who has frozen to death. This conversation takes place as he and Jane are walking home from school, and they have to step off the street to make way for a funeral procession.

Thus, the structure of the viewer's experience of this cinematic moment is one in which God is described aurally and equated to beauty as death drives by, and then beauty is shown visually as a plastic bag—perhaps the most trivial and discardable element of our consumer culture—on screen. In redeeming these symbols, the Fitts character reveals with his words the wisdom of medieval Christianity.

Johan Huizinga describes this medieval wisdom of looking into the inward significance of visible things as follows:

---

[34] *American Beauty*, directed by Sam Mendes (Glendale, CA: DreamWorks SKG, 1999), DVD, emphasis added.

The Middle Ages never forgot that all things would be absurd, if their meaning were exhausted in their function and their place in the phenomenal world, if by their essence they did not reach into a world beyond this. This idea of a deeper significance in ordinary things is familiar to us as well, independently of religious convictions: as an indefinite feeling which may be called up at any moment, by the sound of raindrops on the leaves or by the lamplight on a table. Such sensations may take the form of a morbid oppression, so that all things seem to be charged with a menace or a riddle which we must solve at any cost. Or they may be experienced as a source of tranquility and assurance, by filling us with the sense that our own life, too, is involved in this hidden meaning in the world.[35]

The Medievals got their understanding through the images, which were a form of visual or folk literacy based on the more complex phonetic literacy required to understand Scripture. But they looked through both visual analogical images (i.e., art, icons, etc.) to see the higher truth of Scripture, which also encouraged them to look through reality as but a shadow of the ideal, or the heavenly realm. In their context, it was only when the symbolic environment of the cathedral became saturated with images that they took on the role of entertainment, of distraction from the very see-through quality they were meant to engender. In a way, then, one could argue that the effect of the iconoclasts was to help restore perceptual balance to the faithful. What many now see as overdoing it in the destruction of images can be understood as an aural hyperbolic response to a visually hyperbolic situation.

In *Art and Beauty in the Middle Ages*, Umberto Eco points to the grander scheme into which the character Ricky Fitts has placed himself:

The Medievals inhabited a world filled with references, reminders, and overtones of Divinity, manifestations of God in things.

---

[35] Johan Huizinga, *The Waning of the Middle Ages*, ed. F. Hopman (New York: St. Martins Press, 1967), 194.

Nature spoke to them heraldically: lions or nut-trees were more than they seemed; griffins were just as real as lions because, like them, they were signs of a higher truth.[36]

In *American Beauty*, Ricky's words are the substructure on top of which the visual images make sense. With the film's dialogue muted, both of these scenes lose all of their power, wonder, and beauty.

In its cultural context, *American Beauty* was a completely secular film that neither espoused nor represented religiosity in any of its characters' lives, yet it won the top honors at the Academy Awards that year and was consistently called a highly spiritual film. Gregor Goethals describes the triumph of the spirituality of secular media over Christian media: "Secular culture is popular, not because it is secular, but perhaps because it is sacramental."[37]

The Medievals looked through rather than at their world as being emblematic of the deeper goodness, beauty, and truth of God and the schema of the world he had created. Modern secular Hollywood does this same thing without being labeled religious. Our task as Christians, then, may be to remember that Jesus Christ is, in McLuhan's words, "the one case where we can say that the medium and the message are fully one and the same," and as he reminded us, "the process of perception is that of incarnation."[38] Our visual media and our aural media must work in such a way as not to merely reflect the viewer's own narcissistic image back to himself, as so much art does today, but to refract the light in such a way that he sees something beyond himself, and beyond his imagination, to the image of the One who is invisible, unspeakable, and ineffable, and yet the source of all our imaginings.

If this is valid, then Scripture should confirm it. And I think we find confirmation in Exodus 25:18–22:

[36] Umberto Eco, *Art and Beauty in the Middle Ages*, trans. Hugh Bredin (New Haven, CT: Yale University Press, 2002), 53.

[37] Gregor Goethals, *The TV Ritual: Worship at the Video Altar* (Boston: Beacon Press, 1981), 143.

[38] McLuhan, McLuhan, and Szklarek, *The Medium and the Light*, 102.

And make two cherubim out of hammered gold at the ends of the cover. Make one cherub on one end and the second cherub on the other; make the cherubim of one piece with the cover, at the two ends. The cherubim are to have their wings spread upward, overshadowing the cover with them. The cherubim are to face each other, looking toward the cover. Place the cover on top of the ark and put in the ark the tablets of the covenant law that I will give you. There, above the cover between the two cherubim that are over the ark of the covenant law, I will meet with you and give you all my commands for the Israelites. (NIV)

In this description, God is literally framed by art. He is seen not in the gold cherubim, but through them, or to be more precise, between the two cherubim facing each other. The testimony of his word is underneath the image, the way a caption or title makes sense of a picture. The word *medium* means precisely "that which goes between." As Christ is our Mediator, our Medium, and our Maker, and as he points us to the Father, so too should all our artwork, all our applications of our God-given imagination, be eternally vigilant in pointing not at our art, but through it to the invisible between our art, framed by our art, arrived at through our art.

The early church understood this well with its reversal of perspective and other artistic elements when creating icons. According to Constantine Cavarnos, the seven functions of Orthodox icons are these:

(1) They enhance the beauty of the church. (2) They instruct us in matters pertaining to the Christian faith. (3) They remind us of this faith. (4) They lift us up to the prototypes which they symbolize, to a higher level of thought and feeling. (5) They arouse us to imitate the virtues of the holy personages depicted on them. (6) They help to transform us, to sanctify us. (7) They serve as a means of worship and veneration.[39]

---

[39] Constantine Cavarnos, *Orthodox Iconography* (Belmont: The Institute for Byzantine and Modern Greek Studies, 1977), 30.

Nowhere in this list of seven functions are icons intended to (a) accurately represent the objects or persons depicted, or (b) enhance our visual perception of what and who these things were in history. Instead, through the use of specifically anti-realist and anti-representational techniques, these visual images are of an artistic tradition that specifically invite us to see *through them* rather than merely rest our eyes on their surface. Though we cannot derive from this a prescriptive catalog of acceptable versus unacceptable use of visual media by and for Christian witness, it does, I think, offer us a descriptive glimpse of how our use of visual media ought to be conceived.

In one sense, Orthodox icons are perhaps the earliest version of René Magritte's painting *The Treachery of Images*, which pictured a pipe with the slogan "*Ceci n'est pas une pipe*" ("This is not a pipe") to remind the viewer that despite being representational and realistic, this was in fact a mediated pipe, merely a painting of a pipe. The painting cannot become for us the "true reality" of Durant's inward significance until we see through its surface. The words underneath Magritte's image help us remember—and like the Ricky Fitts character in *American Beauty*, Christians *need* to remember.

The icon says this same thing implicitly, without using words: Do not look at this, for this is not the Christ; this is an icon of the Good Shepherd, for instance, through which you may meditate on the One who is the true Christ. The New American Standard Bible translation of 1 Corinthians 8:4 tells us, "We know that there is no such thing as an idol in the world"—which seems to reveal two changes in the cultural context: (1) that the Abrahamic rebellion against worshiping gods made by human hands was now no longer of primary concern, because (2) Christians were now able to see through such gods as being existentially unreal. Both of these perceptions could only encourage their belief in the reality of a single, true, living God who is existentially real but visibly imperceptible.

In between the two cherubim of the ark of the covenant, in the nonexistence of idols in the physical world and in the human perceptual inability to literally "see" the gospel with our eyes because we can only ultimately hear it, our imagination must do its work in order for God to meet with us. As Neil Postman put it,

> The God of the Jews was to exist in the Word and through the Word, and unprecedented conception requiring the highest order of abstract thinking.[40]

This is real work, and this is hard work—which is perhaps why Scripture so clearly points us to an understanding of it that requires real humility, as between the difference of a brother with superior knowledge and a brother with lesser knowledge:

> For if others see you—with your "superior knowledge"—eating in the temple of an idol, won't they be encouraged to violate their conscience by eating food that has been offered to an idol? So because of your superior knowledge, a weak believer for whom Christ died will be destroyed. (1 Cor. 8:10–11 NLT)

Significantly, Scripture does not give us the freedom or the obligation to enlighten those without "superior knowledge." There is no education program called for; instead, we are obligated to follow the universal rule of civilization in which the strong defend the weak.

The ear's inherent and essential interiority, then, should be our primary guide when creating and viewing visual media, so that all things may be seen as clearly as possible in their truest sense. Between the point of apprehension and comprehension, between the external stimulus hitting our optic or auditory nerves and our mind's recognition of a deeper, invisible, more real truth, Christians should never be content to let their senses remain on the

---

[40] Postman, *Amusing Ourselves to Death*, 9.

surface and should likewise create media that penetrates beneath the surface of sensory perception. As writing does this naturally and inherently with speech, Christians should likewise do this intentionally and carefully with visual media of analogical symbols: we should create visual media that we can hear the effect of internally.

If the Old Testament insisted that we not make any visual images of God, then today we live in a technological society where visual media imagery has become a competing god for our time and attention and money. Perhaps we can strengthen our witness by guiding our visual-audio culture toward an audio-visual understanding. This should include an implicit understanding of all media forms as pointing to something beyond or beneath themselves, and to an explicit standard of media participation and production that creates from the knowledge that "all things would be absurd, if their meaning were exhausted in their function and their place in the phenomenal world, if by their essence they did not reach into a world beyond this."[41]

We must avoid this absurdity lest the world find us more absurd, and our message less relevant, than we already are and they already do. In reclaiming the lost understanding of the historic church regarding the perception of ear and eye, perhaps conscientious Christians can once again speak meaningfully to those who have ears to hear, and perhaps we can begin to bring some unity to the fragmentation of our "multiple Christianities" and the gazillion-channel universe that perceives them as but frequencies along the entertainment spectrum.

---

[41] Johan Huizinga, quoted in Eco, *Art and Beauty in the Middle Ages*, 52.

4

YOU ARE BEING LIED TO. WHAT IS THE NATURE OF THE LIE?

The key things to remember in all media study is that all media exist within the context of global capitalism, they manifest themselves as corporations, and all of these corporations operate with the identical, ultimate goal of producing an economic return-on-investment for their owners and shareholders. Thus, no matter what point of view, ideology, or philosophy you think you are getting, buying, renting, or subscribing to, the ultimate philosophy of most media is that of profit. In a sense, this is no bigger news than Scripture announcing to you (as it has for millennia) that you cannot serve both God and mammon (cf. Matt. 6:24 KJV; Luke 16:13). In God's economy of nature, based on surplus, there is enough to go around for everyone. (See the book of Acts for how this happened in early Christian communities.) In man's economy of culture, based on scarcity (or the manufactured perception thereof), a person must fight for the "limited resources" that exist in all sectors in order to survive.

Here's a strange, invisible fact of modern life: the automobile kills more people each year (1,240,000 globally) than war and terrorism combined (440,000 globally). So just as it is wise to recognize that getting into your car is the most dangerous thing you do each day, so too is it helpful to remember that when you open a screen, turn on a TV, click a link, or pick up a magazine, whatever else someone is trying to inform, persuade, or entertain you with, they are trying to relieve you of the money in your pocket. So there is always an "agenda" with modern media, and this is first and foremost an economic agenda that has nothing to do with political or religious or philosophical beliefs.

Then too, the agenda has been concentrated, whereas it was once distributed. As the late Turkish-American media critic Ben Bagdikian noted in his 1983 book *The Media Monopoly*, there was an ever-growing concentration of mergers and acquisitions whereby the vast majority of your news, information, and opinions were coming from just fifty sources in the mid-twentieth century. Bagdikian's alarm in 1983 was that what used to produce the "public's right to know" was a vast and broadly based collection of papers and magazines, large and small, all competing for your readership and attention. Now, under television conditions, all that was shrinking. What ultimately horrified Bagdikian in his updated 2000 edition, was the discovery that these fifty media corporations had now merged themselves down to just five! These are the five media corporations that produce your entertainment, your news, your opinions, your culture, your level of public discourse; "they manufacture a social and political world":

Time Warner
Walt Disney (ABC News)
News Corporation (Rupert Murdoch)
Viacom (formerly CBS)
Bertelsmann (Germany)

In close sixth place behind these five is NBC, which is owned by American multinational conglomerate corporation giant General Electric. Five out of the six are American multinational conglomerates, and it is their media product that not only Americans, but also now the whole world, primarily consumes. This is to say nothing of the big digital five (Amazon, Google, Facebook, Apple, and Microsoft), which are soon going to eat the five media corporations for lunch the way Amazon just swallowed Whole Foods. In Europe, for example, the US market share of cinema audiences ranges from 54 to 86 percent.[1] A Parisian in France has a 65 percent chance of watching an American film when going out to the movies and less than a 35 percent of watching a French film (because other countries' films are also playing). No wonder the French describe their free time with the phrase "*le weekend*" instead of the French term "*fin de semaine*."

Now it is still an open question that historians of the future will likely determine, whether an American agenda for global politics, culture, education, and society will produce a new Golden Age or another fall of Rome. But this is the direction that the technology has taken us, and it is to this that we should be paying attention. It just happens to have happened to America, by virtue of our technology. Any country that developed military and civilian technologies (flip sides of the same coin) as rapidly would also find itself in the same position. The historical syllogism is very simple:

> History is written by winners.
> Winners are the winners of wars.
> Winning wars requires superior technological capabilities.
> Thus, Team America.

The Internet, like the highway system, is but another military technology leased to citizens in times of peace. The average consumer does not perceive this, but the history of the Internet, from Darpanet down to the NSA, reveals a consistent pattern of control of information on the presupposition that knowledge is power. And by "times of peace" I mean, of course, times of war. Since 1945, the United States has been in a continuous militarized state of war, with the latest being the GWOT, the Global War on Terror.

---

[1] Robert J. Lieber, *The American Era: Power and Strategy for the 21st Century* (Cambridge: Cambridge University Press, 2005), 103–4.

So even though Americans may perceive it as "times of peace," it is anything but.

In World War II, there were roughly 72 countries at war. In 2016, there were 151 countries at war.[2] As Marshall McLuhan put it, "War is never anything less than accelerated technological change."[3] And if technology can determine geopolitics, then it can also play a determining role in psychology, religion, and spirituality itself.

TECHNOLOGY IS THEOLOGY: THE MEDIUM IS THE MESSIAH

Technology is epistemology. That is the theory. Everything else is commentary. The shorthand way to understand this is simply to follow the syllogism down to its roots:

> Everything you are conscious of is predicated on what you are not conscious of.
> Everything you are conscious of comes to you through your perceptions.
> Every perception you have is a function of your five senses.
> Every new technology alters the balance, or "ratio," of your senses.

To regain your senses, you have to go back to the beginning and ask two different but identical questions:

1. Who was I before all this technology took over my life?
2. Who was man before the fall?

A Christian theory of media posits that God made man, his highest organism, and placed him into the perfect environment wherein man could thrive, prosper, and be happy. There was no technology in this environment because, in a perfect world, you

---

[2] For a more nuanced view of this data, see http://economicsandpeace.org/wp-content/uploads/2016/06/GPI-2016-Report_2.pdf.
[3] Marshall McLuhan, *Understanding Media: The Extensions of Man* (New York: McGraw-Hill, 1964), 102.

cannot improve it by inventing any form of labor-saving or time-saving devices. The improvement upon perfection that Adam and Eve sought did not exist, was based on a lie told by the accuser, and only served to imbalance the sense ratios of the original humans. In the garden, the hierarchy of the senses went like this, from most important to least:

> hearing
> seeing
> smelling
> touching
> tasting

The tree of the knowledge of good and evil was made appealing by Satan's appeal to the primacy of the eye over the ear. Prior to this, Adam and Eve walked in the garden and were continuously in the acoustic, but not visual, presence of the Lord. They could hear him. And he could hear them—his curiosity about their ingenuity, in fact, lay only in the very linguistic ability he had given them (and which separated them from the rest of the animals: he wanted to know what Adam would name them).

Satan's promise to Eve offers three parts (Gen. 3:5):

1. Your eyes will be open.
2. You will know good and evil.
3. You will be like God.

And like all great liars, two out of three of these promises did come true: Their eyes were opened. They did know good and evil. But instead of being "like God," they suddenly found themselves naked and ashamed. Whereas before, they were naked and unashamed.

After the fall, the hierarchy of the senses shifted to this:

> seeing
> hearing

smelling
touching
tasting

You can perceive this by watching little children at the beach. The toddler is naked and unashamed to not be wearing a diaper. Anyone over three years old is ridiculously self-conscious about being naked.

Students without their iPhones? "I feel naked without it." This is a theological statement: the Hebrew word for *atonement* is the same as the word for *covering*.

Digital media technology is simply the fourth and latest stage of technological development (after writing, printing, and electricity), and it too promises a similar threefold Godlikeness:

1. You will be omniscient.
2. You will be omnipresent.
3. You will be omnipotent.

Thanks to the smartphone and a reliable Wi-Fi signal, now almost all of us carry in our very pockets the tools of portable omniscience and omnipresence. But two out of these three have not yet added up to omnipotence, and the evidence suggests that it is not only not granting us the power of a god, but it seems to be robbing us of our very finite but very real human dignity, identity, history, and purpose.

Ever after Adam and Eve traded an ear for an eye, they and their descendants were reminded that "faith comes from hearing" (Rom. 10:17) and that "faith is . . . the evidence of things not seen" (Heb. 11:1 KJV).

When Abraham left home and went west to the land of Canaan, he perceived for the first time that a change in faith would necessarily be accompanied by a change in media forms of worship: he traded the gods of stone and wood for the invisible God of gods.

When Moses led the Israelites out of Egypt, he led them through forty years in the wilderness, with a significant stop at Mount Sinai. Here he received the Ten Commandments, which some scholars suggest was also the birth of the Hebrew alphabet—an exchange of the Egyptian pictographic writing system for an abstract, phoneme-based writing system. The squiggles evolved to no longer "look like" the things they represented; now they represented abstract noises that the human mouth could make, and it took another layer of completion before you could make certain sounds arrive at certain meanings. The second commandment God gave to ensure this new identity was a law that connected communication style with moral outcome: henceforth, thou shalt not use any pictographic symbol systems; it will bias you toward idolatry.

This means that *God cares about the forms of the media technologies we use as much or more than the content*. For New Testament examples, consider that even Paul pointed out that speech was life-giving while writing tended to produce a hardening of the perceptual categories: ". . . for the letter kills, but the Spirit gives life" (2 Cor. 3:6). Our Lord Jesus Christ made this principle profoundly vivid when he liberated the woman who was caught red-handed in adultery. He used the power of the living word—speech—to create a mistrial and thereby free a woman who was already dead in the eyes of her judges, jury, and executioners.

So if you accept that God cares about the form as much as the substance, about the medium as much as the message, about the context as much as the content, then Christians should care what unintended messages they might be sending by simply adopting the newest, the latest, the fastest, and the most efficient technologies in the name of Christ. Digital media technologies already possess, in and of themselves, their own presuppositions, their own effectiveness, and their own epistemology, and cannot be put in the service of Jesus Christ without a certain amount of fear and trembling about their unintended consequences.[4]

Jesus Christ, who is our Mediator, our Medium, and our Messiah, is also the basis of our community, our communication, and our communion. He is the center, source, focus, and purpose of all that we should do. If you have a media or technology-related question, he is the one to ask. In Greek, Jesus was not a carpenter, he was a *tekton*, a master builder (in wood or stone), which is also related to the root word of *architect*. This comes from *tekne*—art or craft—and is the root of the word *technology*. Thus, the second Person of the Trinity is the Master Builder, Architect, and ultimate Maker of the cosmos and all that is in it. He should know a thing or two about how things are made, how they work, and what the design was. Science is just now beginning to catch up to how nature is actually an incredibly sophisticated ecological design system in which the parts all contribute to a whole that is greater than themselves.

Now is the time for Christians to take up a conscious awareness of the unconscious effects of media and communication technologies. Now is the time for the sleepers to awake.

---

[4] Material in this paragraph was largely drawn from my article "The Future of the Church Is Analog, Not Digital," *Christianity Today*, September 23, 2016, http://www.christianitytoday.com/ct/2016/october/future-of-church-is-analog-not-digital.html.

QUESTIONS FOR REFLECTION

I hope thus far that I have been descriptive and not prescriptive. I hope to impart to you the ways in which a Christian ecology of media is, like media ecology in general, very much more interested in questions than in answers. That is how Jacques Ellul understood the Bible itself—not as a series of answers to life's questions, but as a series of questions that asks each of us, in our particular historical circumstance, to answer for our lives to God himself. And so I would like to end this book with a lengthy series of questions written by myself and by others who have come before me. I encourage you to revisit this section and ask yourself at least one of these questions each time you engage in media, journalism, or communication technologies during your life.

1. How much media do you consume? What is your media diet? Keep a daily, weekly, monthly, or yearly journal and log every minute spent with media. You may be surprised by your findings.

2. What do you want to do with your life? How many hours would it take to achieve that level of expertise or excellence in your chosen field? Where can you find those hours? In this exercise, take the number of hours discovered in Question 1 and divide them by the number of hours needed in Question 2. Which number is bigger? Does a selective sacrifice of media intake allow you to achieve your dreams?

3. What media can you fast from? What can you live without?

4. What media are you using? What media are you intentional, rational, and purposeful about? What media forms are disembodied means to embodied ends? What media are you using to actually further the kingdom of God? What media are you passively being used by? What media, if you're honest with yourself, are you lying to yourself about?

5. What is media costing you? Write down your actual costs of cell-phone, data plan, cable, electricity, and other media-related expenses. How much money is that? To what better use could this money be spent? In a world of ubiquitous Wi-Fi hotspots, how much of your media budget could be had for free if you were willing to be slightly inconvenienced?

6. Who in your immediate circle of family, friends, and loved ones could use a visit right now from you? Who could use one tonight? Later this week? How can you "put it down" in order to "take it up" in person with the people you care about?

7. What media are you making? Are you retweeting? Are you posting on a blog? Are you making a vine? A YouTube video? A film? Writing a book? Think about the return on investment of your time. Does it take you more time to photograph your food than to eat it? Is there a better way to spend your time? If you are making something significant, worthwhile, and of value, to whom and for what purposes will it be put? A whole lot of "wasted effort" can be avoided up-front by simply and honestly assessing these factors and "counting the cost."

8. What can you make that will help your neighbor? What can you make that will help, in Wendell Berry's phrase, "a woman who is near to giving birth"? What media can you make that will help your audience to hear the still, small voice of God?

9. Where are you right now? Are you here? Or are you there? Are you in the room you are in, with the people in it? Or are you physically present but emotionally absent? Do you have "anywhere is better than here" syndrome? When you are in Paris, do you wish you were in New York? When in Manhattan, do you look for French cafes? What role does media play in creating the constant dissatisfaction with where you are right now and what you are doing right now?

10. You can't keep up. But you can stay tuned. How can you sacri-

fice media in order to pay more attention to media? How can you save 35 hours a week by not watching TV in order to read the few really good books that are among the three hundred thousand published each year? How can you use good media habits to displace bad media habits?

11. You want it all? Now? Really? How has media created in you a voracious desire to consume, know, and understand everything? How did omniscience go from being a trait of God alone to being your natural-born right as a digital citizen? And how can you use media to combat this insanely impossible task in order to acquire the knowledge, skill, and wisdom to become very, very good at a few select things?

12. The Internet is information is knowledge is power. Yet the highest spiritual calling has always been humility. How will you use digital media technologies to enhance not your knowledge, pride, and power, but your servant's heart, your humble wisdom, your deference to others as better than yourself?

13. You look fat/skinny/tall/short/pretty/ugly in that. Social media places an enormous emphasis on the body as pure digital information, and the social costs and peer pressure are enormous. Eighty percent of American eleven-year-old girls are on a diet, according to Jean Kilbourne. How will you use digital media not to look better but to sound better, to speak softer, and to show the love of God in your voice and your actions?

14. Rebellion against the cultural norm is just a tattoo parlor away. Why not some bodily modifications? If you're under age forty, chances are statistically pretty high that you already are tattooed, pierced, or dyed in some creative style[1]—and in a place or way that your parents or grandparents would never have dreamed of—

---

[1] According to Pew Research, 36 percent of Generation Y and 40 percent of Gen X have a tattoo. See "Tattooed Gen Nexters," Fact Tank, Pew Research Center, December 9, 2008, http://www.pew research.org/daily-number/tattooed-gen-nexters/.

thanks to the overwhelming emphasis that digital media places on the visual. In what ways are digital media actually reinforcing body modification as a corollary to the emphasis on the visual?

15. The sin of despair (literally, *to lose hope*) is on the rise. Suicide surpassed homicide, car crashes, and war as the leading cause of death among American youth in the past ten years. The future belongs to those who can create a future by making a family and producing offspring. In what ways has digital media enhanced or destroyed your vision for your own personal future? What media habits might be worth changing to increase your hope and decrease your despair?

16. Essentially 5,778 years of human history have gone by without needing modern technology. Why do you need it now? Can you imagine living a day, a week, a month, or a year without new technology? Can you imagine living your whole life without it? What will be gained or lost by making such a decision?

17. What does technology do? What does it undo? In what ways will you use it? In what ways will it use you? Is it your master, or your slave, or your equal?

In addition to these questions, here are six questions[2] that Neil Postman thought should be asked of any new technology:

1. What is the problem to which this technology is the solution?
2. Whose problem is it?
3. What new problems might be created by solving the original problem?
4. Which people and what institutions will be most seriously harmed by this new technology?

---

[2] These questions show up variously as five, six, or seven questions that Neil Postman asks and are all derived from his book *Technopoly: The Surrender of Culture to Technology* (New York: Alfred A Knopf, 1992), which is highly recommended.

5. What changes in language are being forced by this new technology?
6. What sort of people and institutions gain special economic and political power from this new technology?

And finally, here are Jacques Ellul's "77 Reasonable Questions to Ask about Any Technology,"[3] grouped by theme:

ECOLOGICAL

1. What are its effects on the health of the planet and of the person?
2. Does it preserve or destroy biodiversity?
3. Does it preserve or reduce ecosystem integrity?
4. What are its effects on the land?
5. What are its effects on wildlife?
6. How much, and what kind of, waste does it generate?
7. Does it incorporate the principles of ecological design?
8. Does it break the bond of renewal between humans and nature?
9. Does it preserve or reduce cultural diversity?
10. What is the totality of its effects, its "ecology"?

SOCIAL

1. Does it serve community?
2. Does it empower community members?
3. How does it affect our perception of our needs?
4. Is it consistent with the creation of a communal, human economy?
5. What are its effects on relationships?
6. Does it undermine conviviality?
7. Does it undermine traditional forms of community?
8. How does it affect our way of seeing and experiencing the world?
9. Does it foster a diversity of forms of knowledge?

---

[3] Jacques Ellul's questions are reprinted in Jeffrey Greenman, Read Mercer Schuchardt, and Noah Toly, *Understanding Jacques Ellul* (Eugene, OR: Wipf and Stock, 2011).

10. Does it build on, or contribute to, the renewal of traditional forms of knowledge?
11. Does it serve to commodity knowledge or relationships?
12. To what extent does it redefine reality?
13. Does it erase a sense of time and history?
14. What is its potential to become addictive?

PRACTICAL

1. What does it make?
2. Who does it benefit?
3. What is its purpose?
4. Where was it produced?
5. Where is it used?
6. Where must it go when it's broken or obsolete?
7. How expensive is it?
8. Can it be repaired?
9. Can an ordinary person repair it?

MORAL

1. What values does its use foster?
2. What is gained by its use?
3. What are its effects beyond its utility to the individual?
4. What is lost in using it?
5. What are its effects on the least advantaged in society?

ETHICAL

1. How complicated is it?
2. What does it allow us to ignore?
3. To what extent does it distance agent from effect?
4. Can we assume personal or communal responsibility for its effects?
5. Can its effects be directly apprehended?
6. What ancillary technologies does it require?
7. What behavior might it make possible in the future?
8. What other technologies might it make possible?
9. Does it alter our sense of time and relationships in ways conducive to nihilism?

VOCATIONAL

1. What is its impact on craft?
2. Does it reduce, deaden, or enhance human creativity?
3. Is it the least-imposing technology available for the task?
4. Does it replace, or does it aid, human hands and human beings?
5. Can it be responsive to organic circumstance?
6. Does it depress or enhance the quality of goods?
7. Does it depress or enhance the meaning of work?

METAPHYSICAL

1. What aspect of the inner self does it reflect?
2. Does it express love?
3. Does it express rage?
4. What aspect of our past does it reflect?
5. Does it reflect cyclical or linear thinking?

POLITICAL

1. Does it concentrate or equalize power?
2. Does it require or institute a knowledge elite?
3. Is it totalitarian?
4. Does it require a bureaucracy for its perpetuation?
5. What legal empowerments does it require?
6. Does it undermine traditional moral authority?
7. Does it require military defense?
8. Does it enhance or serve military purposes?
9. How does it affect warfare?
10. Is it massifying?
11. Is it consistent with the creation of a global economy?
12. Does it empower transnational corporations?
13. What kind of capital does it require?

AESTHETIC

1. Is it ugly?
2. Does it cause ugliness?
3. What noise does it make?
4. What pace does it set?
5. How does it affect the quality of life (as distinct from the standard of living)?

GLOSSARY

Communication. The art of making many one. Considered a social science by some, *communication* shares the same root as *community*, *communion*, and *communism*. While there are thirty-two theories (or more) about communication, most theories of communication go back to Claude Shannon and Warren Weaver, whose original "transmission model" held that *communication is a source encoding a message along a channel to an intended receiver who decodes it with minimal noise.* Marshall McLuhan called this a "transportation model" and said that he was much more interested in his "transformation model" that looked at what the medium (or channel) of communication did to transform the meaning, rhetoric, location, and identity of the user. This book has been written from the media-ecology model's perspective.

Communication studies. This is the study of various communication media forms, usually a combination of history, theory, and practice, that most typically got their start at the beginning of the radio age. It was deemed urgently necessary by the end of World War II, when scholars understood that German citizens had been persuaded—through propaganda in mass-media forms—to commit great atrocities "for the good of the nation." The power of mass media in influencing an otherwise educated and refined civilization to such brutality was something that educators realized needed to be prevented in the future through a countercultural program of studying the forms of mass media and communication. Thus, one of the key benefits of studying communication is that it gives the student the tools to perceive whether he is being lied to, propagandized, or otherwise manipulated by the state, the market, the church, or technology itself.

Journalism. Until recently, this referred to the daily newspapers, or "journals" of the day. Today, journalism is in both a free fall and a radical transformation into what is better (though awkwardly) termed *hourlism*, *minutelism*, or *secondlism* by virtue of the speed with which the news is produced and arrives on a screen. *Minutiaelism* seems perhaps like a dismissive term, but is suggested as a replacement term for *journalism* because of the ways that (a) small details of the story come immediately to us, often before the story is complete, (b) these facts can seem trivial in the aftermath of the big event (the way 9/11 was first reported by the AP as a small plane accidentally veering off course into the World Trade Center), and (c) if you pay attention to the news "by the minute" on a newsfeed for twelve hours, by the end of the day you are more distracted, less informed, and filled with *minutiae*. In traditional newspapers, the lead sentence would start with, "Yesterday in New York . . ." as today's news was actually yesterday's event. Under digital assumptions, most news stories start with some variation of, "Reports are pouring in that . . ."

Liberal arts. The *artes liberals* were originally those subjects worthy and essential for a free person to know in order to participate in civic life, such as debating in public, defending yourself in court, serving on a jury, and doing your military service. They were the opposite of the servile arts (*artes vulgares*). The seven liberal arts are: (1) grammar, (2) logic, (3) rhetoric, (4) math, (5) geometry, (6) music, and (7) astronomy.

Media. Plural of *medium*, that which goes between. A medium shirt, a medium steak, and a medium of oil paint are all different, though they all contain this aspect of "in-betweenness." The first two are obvious: a medium shirt is one that is between small and large; a medium steak is a piece of meat cooked between rare and well done. But oil paint is not a medium that is between water color and graphite pencil; rather, it is the chosen medium through which the artist displays his or her expression. So typically, mass media are those "mediums" through which we frame, filter, and interpret reality. This is an especially crucial activity for Christians to engage in studying because Jesus Christ, as the second person of the Trinity, as wholly man and wholly God, is also our *medium*, between God and mankind. It is more complicated by the fact that he is the *unmediating* Mediator, in whom we become one with the Father, and through whom the mediation of the high priest's sacrifice is done away with. "Whoever has seen me has seen the Father" is one way that Christ reveals this paradoxical nature to us (John 14:9).

Media ecology. The study of media as environments. The social-science discipline was created by Neil Postman in 1968, having been inspired by Marshall McLuhan, Jacques Ellul, Walter Ong, and a host of others. The term "media ecology" was coined in late February/early March of 1968, and was first used in a public address by Postman on Sunday, November 24, 1968, at a Teachers of English Conference in Madison, Wisconsin. It evolved into two schools: the "Toronto School," with McLuhan as the chair of the Centre for Culture and Technology, and the "New York School," with Postman as the chair of the Department of Culture and Communication.

Servile arts. The term *artes vulgares* (vulgar arts) evolved to the *artes servile* (servile arts) and finally to the *artes mechanicae* (mechanical arts) precisely because of the changing class consciousness about masters and slaves in various cultural contexts. In today's language, we would call it vocational school, technical school, vo-tech, or community college. The original seven *artes vulgares* were (1) *vestiaria* (tailoring/weaving), (2) *agricultura* (agriculture), (3) *architectura* (architecture/masonry), (4) *militia* and *venatoria* (warfare/military education/"martial arts" and hunting), (5) *mercatura* (trade), (6) *coquinaria* (cooking), and (7) *metallaria* (blacksmithing/metallurgy). Or in other words: (1) clothing, (2) farming, (3) architecture, (4) weaponry, (5) business, (6) cooking, and (7) metalworking.

RESOURCES FOR FURTHER STUDY

American Beauty. Directed by Sam Mendes. Glendale, CA: DreamWorks SKG, 1999. DVD.

Barrett, David, George Kurian, and Todd Johnson. *World Christian Encyclopedia: A Comparative Survey of Churches and Religions in the Modern World*. Oxford: Oxford University Press, 2001.

Baudrillard, Jean. *Simulacra and Simulation*. Translated by Sheila Faria Glaser. Ann Arbor, MI: University of Michigan Press, 1995.

Blake, William. "The Everlasting Gospel." In *The Complete Poetry and Prose of William Blake*. Edited by David Erdman, 520. Oakland: University of California Press, 2008.

———. "A Vision of the Last Judgment." In *Complete Writings*. Edited by Geoffrey Keynes, 604–17. Oxford: Oxford University Press, 1972.

Bureau of Labor Statistics. "American Time Use Survey Summary." Accessed June 24, 2016. http://www.bls.gov/news.release/atus.nr0.htm.

Cavarnos, Constantine. *Orthodox Iconography*. Belmont: The Institute for Byzantine and Modern Greek Studies, 1977.

Chesterton, G. K. *The Everlasting Man*. New York: Image, 1955.

Committee to Protect Journalists. "1,218 Journalists Killed since 1992." Accessed November 18, 2016. https://www.cpj.org/killed/.

Debord, Guy. *The Society of the Spectacle*. Translated by Donald Nicholson-Smith. New York: Zone, 1995.

Durant, Will. *The Story of Philosophy: The Lives and Opinions of the Great Philosophers of the Western World*. New York: Simon and Schuster, 2005. (Originally published in 1926.)

Eco, Umberto. *Art and Beauty in the Middle Ages*. Translated by Hugh Bredin. New Haven, CT: Yale University Press, 2002.

———. *Turning Back the Clock*. London: Vintage Random House, 2008.

Ellul, Jacques. *The Humiliation of the Word*. Translated by Joyce Main Hanks. Grand Rapids, MI: Eerdmans, 1985.

———. *Propaganda: The Formation of Men's Attitudes*. Translated by Konrad Kellen and Jean Lerner, 231. New York: Vintage, 1965.

Emerson, Ralph Waldo. *Complete Prose Works of Ralph Waldo Emerson*. Whitefish, MT: Kessinger, 2007.

Goethals, Gregor. *The TV Ritual*. Boston: Beacon Press, 1981.

Goldman, David. "These Data Miners Know Everything about You." CNN Money, December 16, 2010. http://money.cnn.com/galleries/2010/technology/1012/gallery.data_miners/index.html.

Huizinga, Johan. *The Waning of the Middle Ages*. Translated by F. Hopman. New York: St. Martins Press, 1967. (Originally published in 1924.)

Kalogeropoulos, Demitrios. "The Average American Watches This Much TV Every Day: How Do You Compare?" *The Motley Fool*, March 15, 2015. http://www.fool.com/investing/general/2015/03/15/the-average-american-watches-this-much-tv-every-da.aspx.

Klepeis, Neil. "The National Human Activity Pattern Survey (NHAPS): A Resource for Assessing Exposure to Environmental Pollutants." *Journal of Exposure Analysis & Environmental Epidemiology* 11 (February 6, 2001): 231–52. http://www.nature.com/jes/journal/v11/n3/full/7500165a.html.

Kubey, Robert William, and Mihaly Csikszentmihalyi. *Television and the Quality of Life: How Viewing Shapes Everyday Experience.* Mahwah, NJ: Lawrence Erlbaum, 1990.

Kunstler, James Howard. *The Geography of Nowhere: The Rise and Decline of America's Man-Made Landscape.* New York: Free Press, 1994.

LaFrance, Adrienne. "How Many Websites Are There?" *The Atlantic*, September 30, 2015. http://www.theatlantic.com/technology/archive/2015/09/how-many-websites-are-there/408151/.

Lieber, Robert J. *The American Era: Power and Strategy for the 21st Century.* Cambridge: Cambridge University Press, 2005.

Logan, Robert. *The Alphabet Effect: The Impact of the Phonetic Alphabet on the Development of Western Civilization.* New York: St. Martin's Press, 1987.

MacHugh, Edward. *Edward MacHugh's Treasury of Gospel Hymns and Poems.* Chicago: The Rodeheaver, Hall-Mack Company, 1938.

McLuhan, Marshall. *The Gutenberg Galaxy.* Toronto: University of Toronto Press, 1962.

———. *The Medium and the Light: Reflections on Religion.* Edited by Eric McLuhan and Jacek Szklarek. Toronto: Stoddart, 1999.

———. *Understanding Media: The Extensions of Man.* New York: McGraw-Hill, 1964.

———. *The Video McLuhan, Tape 2: 1965–1970.* VHS. Toronto: McLuhan Productions 1996.

MovieWeb. "2015 Movies." Accessed December 30, 2015. http://movieweb.com/movies/2015/.

National Sleep Foundation. "Annual Sleep in America Poll Exploring Connections with Communications Technology Use and Sleep." March 7, 2011. https://sleepfoundation.org/media-center/press-release/annual-sleep-america-poll-exploring-connections-communications-technology-use-.

Ong, Walter J. *Orality and Literacy: The Technologizing of the Word.* New York: Routledge, 1982.

O'Reilly, Lara. "Netflix Is Eating TV's Dinner: If It Were a TV Network It Would Be at Least the Fourth-Biggest in the US." *Business Insider*, April 16, 2015. http://www.businessinsider.com/average-daily-netflix-usage-according-to-btig-research-2015-4.

Palahniuk, Chuck. *Fight Club.* New York: Henry Holt and Company, 1996.

Plotz, David. "We Are in a Golden Age for Journalism." *National Post*, May 27, 2014. http://news.nationalpost.com/full-comment/david-plotz-we-are-in-a-golden-age-for-journalism.

Postman, Neil. *Amusing Ourselves to Death*. New York: Viking Penguin, 1985.

"Print Dead at 1,803." *The Onion* 49, no. 30 (July 25, 2013). http://www.theonion.com/article/print-dead-at-1803-33244.

Rainie, Lee, and Andrew Perrin. "Slightly Fewer Americans Are Reading Print Books, New Survey Finds." Pew Research Center, October 19, 2015. http://www.pewresearch.org/fact-tank/2015/10/19/slightly-fewer-americans-are-reading-print-books-new-survey-finds/.

Renzenbrink, Tessel. "How Much Electricity Does the Internet Use?" *Elektor*, June 13, 2013. https://www.elektormagazine.com/articles/how-much-electricity-does-the-internet-use.

Rivera, Jaime. "The Total Cost of Ownership for an iPhone 5 Is $1,800." *Pocket Now*, October 3, 2012. http://pocketnow.com/2012/10/03/the-total-for-an-iphone-5-is-1800.

Robinson, Andrew. *The Last Man Who Knew Everything*. St. Paul: Pioneer Press, 2006.

Schulte, Brigid. "Making Time for Kids? Study Says Quality Trumps Quantity." *Washington Post*, March 28, 2015. https://www.washingtonpost.com/local/making-time-for-kids-study-says-quality-trumps-quantity/2015/03/28/10813192-d378-11e4-8fce-3941fc548f1c_story.html.

Shlain, Leonard. *The Alphabet Versus the Goddess*. New York: Viking Press, 1998.

Singer, Katie. "The Real Amount of Energy Used to Power the Internet." *An Electronic Silent Spring*, January 28, 2015. http://www.electronicsilentspring.com/real-amount-energy-power-internet/.

Statista. "Average Time Spent with Major Media per Day in the United States as of April 2016." April 2016. http://www.statista.com/statistics/276683/media-use-in-the-us/.

Vanhoozer, Kevin J. "The Drama of the Christ: The Gospel as Thing Done and Word Made." Presentation at the Gospel and the Imagination Conference, Wheaton College, Wheaton, IL, April 23–26, 2008.

Watzlawick, Paul, Janet Beavin, and Don Jackson, *Pragmatics of Human Communication: A Study of Interactional Patterns, Pathologies, and Paradoxes*. New York: W. W. Norton, 1967.

Wernick, Adam. "In Brazil, Indigenous Tribes Are Still Struggling to Protect the Rainforest—and Their Culture." PRI, March 10, 2014. http://www.pri.org/stories/2014-03-10/brazil-indigenous-tribes-are-still-struggling-protect-rainforest-and-their.

Worldometers. "New Book Titles Published This Year." Accessed August 29, 2017. http://www.worldometers.info/books/.

Wurman, Richard Saul. *Information Anxiety*. New York: Doubleday, 1989.

GENERAL INDEX

SCRIPTURE INDEX

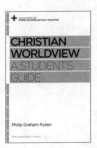
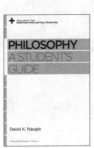
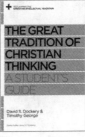
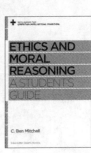

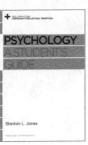

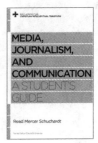